O. J.
The Education of
a Rich Rookie

O.J.
The Education of
a Rich Rookie

by O. J. SIMPSON
with PETE AXTHELM

THE MACMILLAN COMPANY

Copyright © 1970 by O.J. Simpson

The Macmillan Company
866 Third Avenue, New York, N.Y. 10022
Collier-Macmillan Canada Ltd., Toronto, Ontario

Library of Congress Catalog Card Number: 70-126191

FIRST PRINTING

Printed in the United States of America

For
Arnelle and Megan

Contents

Chapter One

A Question of Image

I am twenty-two years old, black, and lucky enough to be very talented at running with a football. In the year or so since I concluded my college career at the University of Southern California, I have earned as much money and made as many good friends as anyone could hope for. I have also suffered some bitter disappointments. I was not as good a rookie professional football player as I had wanted to be; my team, the Buffalo Bills, did not have a good season. But my difficulties in pro ball taught me a lot—about the sport, about people, about myself. I'd be lying if I said that losing was a more enriching experience than winning. I expect to be a winner next year and enjoy it twice as much. Yet my struggles and problems have definitely been educational. And as I realized from my first days with the Bills, education is what being a rookie is all about.

I have been praised, kidded, and criticized about being image-conscious. And I plead guilty to the charge. I have always wanted to be liked and respected; recognition has been far more important to me than money. Coming from a man who has signed contracts worth $900,000 in the past year, this may sound like an empty statement. But my oldest friends know how true it is. And most of them understand why.

I grew up on Connecticut Street in the Patero Hill section of San Francisco. It was not the biggest or poorest or most explosive ghetto in the United States, but it didn't have to be. It still had all the problems and hustles and pain necessary to shape—or twist—the personality of every kid in it. I saw hundreds of those kids lose themselves in the hectic, anonymous struggle for survival; I saw too many take the easiest escape for black people in this society by making themselves faceless and invisible. The ghetto makes you want to hide your real identity—from cops, from teachers, and even from yourself. And it forces you to build up false images—humble or swaggering, casual or tough—in order to handle your enemies and impress your friends.

I tried all the images. I stole hubcaps and started fights to prove my guts to other guys. I crashed dances and parties to show the girls what a big man I was. When I couldn't afford a jacket to wear my high school football letter on, I acted as if a letter jacket just wasn't the cool thing to have. Once I was dragged into jail for taking part in a street skirmish that—in those calmer times— shocked the police enough for them to call it a riot. At the station house they asked me my name. "Burt Lancaster," I blurted out. And since I had no identification, the cops believed me; they never were able to report my actions to my mother or my school. I remember how proud I felt as I watched the cop spell out "Burt Lancaster" on his official form. I was really putting one over, a teenage black kid fooling the Establishment into accepting a fake identity. And I can understand how others got the same feeling of achievement, and kept right on fooling people—and themselves—for the rest of their lives.

But I was lucky; sometimes it stuns me to realize just *how* lucky. I could run faster than anyone around. I was big and strong and agile. So I could dream of becoming a star baseball player like my cousin Ernie Banks. And later, when I happened to try out for football at Galileo High School, I could start thinking of a football career. Scoring touchdowns and listening to crowds cheer, I had reason to be proud that I was O.J. Simpson. And I also had reason to make being O.J. Simpson something to be proud of.

It took a lot of time for the lesson to sink in. I still wanted to shoot craps and hustle around the streets; a few times, I came very close to being tossed off football teams —and if I had left football, I would have left school. After high school, in fact, I was still confused enough about who I was to seriously consider enlisting in the army instead of going to San Francisco City College. But somehow I made all the right decisions, with the aid of some coaches, advisers, and good friends, as well as a girl named Marquerite Whitley. Marquerite was everything I wasn't—square and church-going and middle class. But she was also good-looking and as interested as anyone ever had been in what happened to me, and so I listened when she kept preaching about staying in school. I married her during my first year at USC.

When I started breaking all kinds of scoring records at San Francisco and at USC, then, I became very aware of my image. After taking so long to find out who I was, I didn't want anyone else to misunderstand me. I didn't want to be O.J. Simpson, running back. I wanted to be O.J. Simpson, a good guy. I'm happy to admit it: I really enjoyed being liked. I loved it when kids stopped me for autographs, I loved it when people recognized me on the street. I loved it, I think, because I could at last recognize myself.

I really benefited from all that image-building during the past year. Some athletes have complained that sports-writers and fans are front runners, ready to drop you the minute you run into trouble. Yet when it became clear that I wasn't going to break the American Football League apart with my running, and when the Bills dropped into the second division, people never lost patience with me. I think that people paid me back for some of the excitement and cooperation I had given them in college; and I'm determined to reward them for their patience.

Needless to say, my popularity has also been a key to my financial success. I'm well aware that others have run just as fast and far without ever earning a fraction of the endorsement money I made in the last year. I'm also aware that I have been accused of playing the Estab-lishment game, trying to get important people to like me in order to further my career. That just isn't true. I'm enjoying the money, the big house, the cars; what ghetto kid wouldn't? But I don't feel that I'm being selfish about it. In the long run, I feel that my advances in the business world will shatter a lot of white myths about black ath-letes—and give some pride and hope to a lot of young blacks. And when I'm finished with the challenges of foot-ball, I'm going to take on the challenge of helping black kids in every way I can. I believe that I can do as much for my people in my own way as a Tommie Smith, a Jim Brown, or a Jackie Robinson may choose to do in another way. That's part of the image I want, too.

The trouble with an "image," of course, is that it can give outsiders an unchanging, slightly unreal picture of a man. That's one of the reasons for this book. I want to show some of the changes that I've gone through as a rookie with the Bills. I want to examine the realities of day-to-day life in pro football. I want to describe the excitement and anger and discovery that goes into the education of a rich rookie.

Chapter Two

The Long Summer

When I was drafted by the Bills, I was slow to accept the realities of the situation. Throughout my senior year at USC, I had been asked about my hopes and plans for pro ball, and I had been free with my replies. I told people that I preferred the National League, that I wished I could play in a West Coast city, and that I wanted to make a lot of money. The irrelevance of my comments didn't really sink in, but the fact was that I wouldn't have a bit of choice in the matter. If I wanted to play in the NFL or AFL, I would damn well do it for the team that drafted me.

There was some talk at the time that I might make myself into a test case, fighting the pro draft system in the courts. I never really considered that, but if I had, I would have changed my mind very quickly. Football is a part of my emotional make-up; I thrive on its tension, its challenges, and its thrills. I could no more have waited out a season or two during a court battle than I could have stopped breathing. Early in the summer I wasn't too anxious to start playing because I was caught up in a whirl of public appearances and travels. But when my friends in Los Angeles—Earl McCullouch, Ron Copeland, and Mike Taylor—all took off for camp while I was still unsigned, I really began to get edgy.

My engagements kept me so busy that I didn't have time for regular workouts on my own, so my body felt a bit sluggish—making me all the more impatient to get started. Sometimes I was tempted to sign for anything the Bills offered and get on the next plane to Buffalo. But the temptations were brief. I had worked hard to become the most valuable player in my college class, and I would have degraded myself by taking a lot less than I was worth. There was nothing I could do but wait, fighting my own tensions and hoping for a quick solution to my contract problems. Only one factor made the delay bearable: I had complete trust in the man who was doing the negotiating for me, Chuck Barnes.

Chuck was thirty-eight, but seemed much younger when I first met him; I felt from the start that he was my kind of person and would understand what I needed and wanted. A USC graduate, he had started his Sports Headliners agency only five years earlier, but quickly built it into one of the top organizations in the business of representing sports figures. Since he had worked for the racing division of the Firestone Tire and Rubber Company, his first clients had been auto racers. But he had done a great job for my friend McCullouch when he had signed with the Detroit Lions a year earlier, and it didn't take long for me to see what a job he could do for me.

In our first discussion about money, Chuck and I decided to ask for a package that would include salary, bonus, and a $500,000 loan from the Bills' owner, Ralph Wilson, which we would use for investments and pay back at regular interest rates over four or five years. The loan was the big factor, and added to the other demands, it made it sound as if we were asking for the biggest total payment in football history. But we thought it was feasible because instead of taking a huge bonus and keeping it, we were asking for something that Wilson would get back in full. In Chuck's first meeting with him, Mr. Wilson didn't see it that way. "I'm not in the investment banking business," he told some people. It seemed that he was worried about setting such a precedent. Chuck warned me that we were very far from a settlement, but he added that we were already making headway in setting up some outside income.

I signed my first endorsement contract in the spring, with Chevrolet; it was a shocking experience. I had never really thought about what such contracts meant, and Chuck hadn't even estimated what kind of money I could expect. Then he brought a copy of the contract to me. "The paragraph you'll be interested in," he said casually, "is at the top of the second page."

I gasped when I looked at the figure. For appearing at auto shows, making commercials, and generally lending my name to Chevrolet, I would get more money than I'd ever dreamed of. Over three years, it would amount to a quarter of a million dollars. "God," I said, "you got to be kidding."

"Yes," Chuck said, "it's a good contract."

"Good? It's unbelievable. What the hell can I do to be worth this much to them?"

"Don't worry. They'll be getting their money's worth."

I didn't move for a couple of minutes. It seemed so incredible. I hadn't played a minute of pro ball yet. I hadn't even guessed what Chuck might have been working on. And then boom. All of a sudden, I was in the bucks.

My first exposure to the business world surprised me in another way. John DeLorean, the head of General Motors' Chevrolet division, immediately destroyed any image I had of major executives as stuffy, serious older men. He looked, thought, and talked like a brilliant young guy, and I felt comfortable with him from the start. It was ironic that he was a friend of Ralph Wilson's in Detroit— and he had signed me to a contract long before Wilson.

We had many other offers, but Chuck turned most of them down. He felt that we'd be cheating Chevrolet and cheating ourselves if we started picking up anything less than the best deals. "We'll go first class or not at all," he said, and I knew that we would be going a long way first class. Chuck was getting 10 percent of the money he was making for me, and I was already beginning to think that he was underpaid.

Eventually, we signed two other major contracts, with the American Broadcasting Company and with Royal Crown Cola. The ABC deal was particularly welcome because I was interested in getting into all kinds of acting and television work. The contract was to begin with some appearances on postseason football telecasts, but Roone Arledge, the president of ABC Sports, emphasized that he wanted me to develop an overall television personality. Arledge was known as the most imaginative executive in television sports, and I looked forward to learning under him. I was also anxious to join announcers like Howard Cosell. Howard had often reminded me that he was "the best there was at what he did." And better yet, he happened to be right.

During the off-season, ABC scheduled me to do some interviews and commentary on the *Wide World of Sports* shows, and we also discussed the possibility of a weekend interview show of my own. That didn't work out because my commitments to Chevrolet wouldn't allow me to be in Los Angeles or New York every weekend for tapings; but I was happy that ABC had so many ideas for me. They also planned to give me guest shots on some of their

regular evening shows such as *Mod Squad* and *Bewitched.*
That was fine with me because I had already filmed a
show for CBS called *Medical Center* and found it very
interesting. Somebody had suggested me for a lead role
as a football player with a strange hidden illness. When
I acted out one scene for them, they liked it a lot and
gave me the part. I found it fairly challenging, and things
went so well that the show, originally scheduled as one
of the later episodes in the series, was moved into the
opening slot. The reviews of the show were good, and I've
had several other offers since. Unfortunately I've been too
busy to take on any big acting projects, but eventually
I'll devote more and more time to it. In the meantime, the
more credits I can build up at ABC, the better off I'll be.

The Royal Crown contract wasn't finalized until the season was under way; then it was delayed again because the
week before the deal was supposed to be announced, the
cyclamate controversy broke out. The RC people got so
busy with that problem that they didn't get a chance to
do anything with me during the season. The deal was especially interesting because the RC headquarters is in
Columbus, Georgia; neither Chuck nor I was too confident that a southern-based organization would go for a
big contract with a black athlete. But once again we found
that some major companies were becoming much more
liberal about opening avenues to blacks. In fact, one of
the RC representatives I worked with was Chuck Smith,
a black man; the other was a dynamic executive named
Don Cole.

Altogether, my off-field activities promised to bring me
some $650,000 over several years—not counting the ad-
ditional money I would earn from various appearances
and speaking engagements. And although Ralph Wilson
may not have been thinking that way at the time, those
outside deals put him in a very strong bargaining position. The Chevrolet contract was settled regardless of

where or when I played pro football, but many other arrangements depended in various ways on my signing with the AFL or NFL. Eventually this became a deciding factor in our negotiations, and Chuck and I made concessions that we probably wouldn't have made if football had been my sole source of income. In retrospect, it sometimes seems that the negotiations were almost pointless because in the long run I needed the Bills more than they needed me. At the time, however, I strongly agreed with Chuck that we should stand our ground. I didn't want to begin my new career by devaluing my worth to a team.

Many people believed that our talks with members of the Continental Football League were merely a bluff to let the Bills know that we had alternatives. Yet there were weeks when the Continental League offers seemed almost too good to overlook. From the start, Chuck had said that we would consider all the possibilities, and we gave a lot of thought to the Continental League. To call those offers a bluff would be an insult to the wealthy and sincere men who made them, as well as to Chuck and me.

The best such offer came from the Indianapolis Capitols; the club owners knew Chuck from Indianapolis and they had some long and interesting talks with him. I was surprised to learn that they were very solid people who had both the money and the drive to make the Continental League a success; naturally, they thought that signing me could bring them a long way toward recognition as a major league. Their offer was fantastic—a $500,000 loan that would have extended four years even if I only played for them for one season, a $100,000 bonus, and a salary of $150,000. Both club president Al Savill and league commissioner Jim Dunn convinced me that I could trust them completely. Even if I got hurt or failed to fill as many stadiums as they hoped, I knew I'd get every penny of the money that they promised.

Other offers came from the Fort Worth and Hawaii

franchises of the CFL. Fort Worth promised me $15,000 per game or a percentage of the gate—we would have taken the $15,000. For a fourteen-game season, it would have added up to a record salary. The Hawaii club, we learned, was in trouble and about to be abandoned; but an owner had expressed interest in buying it if he could get me. Finally, there was the Texas millionaire, William Morris, Jr., who offered me a million dollars to sign a personal services contract with him. We never sat and talked with him, but the way I understood it, he would put up the million and then take all profits that I might make for engagements and appearances. I wanted no part of that. He could have had me speaking at a different place every night, trying to get his investment back; for that matter, he could have tried to use me as his personal houseboy if things started going badly.

Ultimately, the Indianapolis offer was the one that we would have taken if we had given up hope on getting a fair deal from the Bills. But the Capitols needed to know in the spring whether we would accept; they would need months to schedule games in bigger stadiums and get the full publicity value out of the deal. As their April deadline approached, Chuck said, "You've got to consider this very carefully." For the first and only time, I had a fleeting doubt about Chuck. I had been convinced from the beginning that he understood my thinking; I had been certain, in other words, that he knew that elements such as prestige and competition were every bit as important to me as money. But when he said that maybe we should consider the Indianapolis deal, I wondered for a moment if he was thinking too much about the money. I told him about my doubts.

"This is a tremendous amount of money, being offered by very good guys," he said. "I wouldn't be acting fair to you if I didn't tell you to think it over very carefully before turning it down."

"You're right," I told him. "It's a hell of an offer and we have to consider it. But I can't get it out of my head that in the Continental League, I'll be more of an entertainer than a competitor. I'm afraid I'd feel more like a traveling circus, or the Harlem Globetrotters, than a genuine football player."

We turned it down, with sincere regrets, and settled down for the long contract battle with the Bills. Gradually we lowered our demands for salary and bonuses, hoping to keep the loan idea alive; after at least one meeting, I got the impression that one of Wilson's advisers was really intrigued by our proposal—but Mr. Wilson obviously didn't agree. Wilson was a gentleman from the first day I met him, and I think his attitude made me confident that we would eventually get things ironed out. But every time I'd start feeling good about the possibilities, I'd read another story quoting him about how "outrageous" our demands were. Training camp opened, the College All-Star game passed, and I was still waiting nervously for an agreement.

Finally, Chuck called me and said that by holding out, we might have been delaying other off-the-field deals that would mean more money than the Buffalo contract, anyway. He said that he didn't want to give in and accept just anything—but he did think that we would have to accept the first offer that we could live with. Finally we settled for a four-year contract worth $250,000 in salary —$55,000 for the first season with a $5,000 increase for each following year. We also got a part of the loan we had sought—$150,000—to be paid back at regular interest rates over the four years. The amounts were supposed to be secret, but estimates immediately appeared in all the papers, and they were so close to the real figures that it was clear that a source near the Bills had leaked them. Apparently they figured that, considering how high we had been aiming, they had gotten us down far enough to

consider it a victory. But Chuck and I weren't worried
about victories or defeats. We had gained a healthy contract, and at last the door was open to other deals—and to
my professional debut.

Some people got a wrong impression about the way we
finally came to terms with the Bills. Wilson was represented at our last negotiating session by a San Diego
lawyer named Don Augustine, who later made some comments that seemed designed to overemphasize his own
role in the settlement. "Without Simpson in the room,"
Augustine said, "I suspect that we never would have ob-
tained an agreement." He added that I had realized that
I "owed more to football than football owed to me." These
statements implied, first, that Chuck was too greedy and
hardheaded to deal with, and second, that I had been
starry-eyed and unrealistic, and Augustine had brought
me down to earth. Neither implication was true, and I
was annoyed that Augustine, a former lawyer for the
AFL Players Association, made any public statements at
all about our private meeting. The fact was that Chuck
and I didn't need anyone or anything to bring us down
to earth. We had looked at our needs realistically and
made up our minds to take the best and quickest deal we
could get. It wouldn't have really mattered very much
whether Wilson, Augustine, or anyone else had done the
final negotiating.

Once the major contracts had been signed, I settled
down to a very pleasant and profitable relationship with
Chuck Barnes and his brother, Bruce, who joined him at
Sports Headliners last year. Chuck, working mainly out of
his Indianapolis office, took care of much of my overall
financial planning; Bruce, in the agency's new Los Angeles office, helped us to set up and furnish our house and
to handle our day-to-day budgets. The two brothers made

an interesting combination. Chuck was serious and intense most of the time, considering every angle of everything we entered into; Bruce was more inclined to see the humor in various situations. Along with Sports Headliners lawyer Dave Lockton, they took most outside pressures from my shoulders and gave me all the advice I needed. I spoke to one or both of them almost every day of the season, and they became good friends of mine as well as business managers. As every paper from the *Sporting News* to the *Wall Street Journal* wrote up my business activities, some readers may have gotten the impression that I was severely overextending myself. But actually, Chuck and Bruce made my entrance into the world of money as simple as it was worthwhile.

It bothered me at times that so much attention was focused on my financial life. Every athlete wants to concentrate mainly on his sport, and wants the public to feel confident that he is devoting himself completely to his job or team. But I understood that all the talk about money was inevitable—and in some ways, I thought it was even beneficial. By being in front of the television camera on so many commercials and appearances, I was shattering a lot of myths for black kids. Blacks too often get conditioned to think that the beautiful cars and houses and luxuries they see in commercials are white people's property; they may see white athletes as all-around businessmen and entertainers, but they see blacks simply as athletes. Growing up black can make you cynical. I can remember when we would look at some good athlete who was struggling along as a playground director or small-time salesman. "He made it big in the sports world," we'd say. "And now what does he have to show for it?" Now I've proven that a black can gain as much from athletics as a white star; and I'd like to think that a few discouraged black kids will think of me when they're on the verge

of giving up hope of using sports to climb out of the
ghetto for good.

Overall, the months between the end of my USC career
and the day I reported to the Bills were the longest, the
most lucrative, and the most confusing of my life. I certainly made a good decision in choosing an agent, and
I entered the world of business and finance with a splash.
But basically I was a football player, and the world that
I was really impatient to enter was pro football. I should
have been preparing for pro ball with more and harder
workouts than I'd ever put together before; yet ironically,
I became so preoccupied with the whirl of contracts, appearances, and negotiations that I hardly worked out at
all. It was a mistake I'll never make again; I actually
reported to Buffalo in the worst shape of my career. So
despite all the new experiences and fortunes I had enjoyed, it was, in the most important sense, a wasted
summer.

Chapter Three

First Impressions

As my plane descended toward the sprawling gray collection of buildings, smokestacks, and frame houses that is Buffalo, New York, I suddenly began to wonder—for the first time, really—just what to expect. I had thought a lot about Buffalo, naturally, ever since it had become clear that the Bills would draft me. My first thought had been in the form of a nightmare, and later I'd made some offhand remarks that probably bothered some Buffalonians. But overall I had felt pretty sanguine about the whole thing. "Any city's okay," I kept telling myself, "as long as you've got enough money to spend in it."

But now that I had the money to spend and was actually on my way into this new territory, I couldn't help worrying. After all, my views on almost anything tend to be fairly pleasant when I'm sitting by a southern California pool or standing alongside the rail at Santa Anita Racetrack with Earl McCullouch, Mike Battle, and my other horseplaying friends from USC. But staring out of a plane window over Buffalo, I started assembling what could have been a strong local case against O.J. Simpson.

I had been told that Buffalo was a hardbitten, hardworking town where people sweated for every dollar they made—and resented anyone who picked up a buck too easily. I also knew that the local fans took their football very seriously, and might not understand how one of their stars could pass up a month of valuable training time in a fight for more money. In the minds of some conservative Buffalonians, I had taken the Bills' popular owner for more than I was worth. And I was a rich and highly publicized newcomer to a team built around solid older men whose names—Tom Sestak and Ron McDole, Harry Jacobs and George Saimes—were a rich part of football legend in a town that needed all the legends it could find. I wasn't sure how Buffalo would greet me.

I needn't have worried at all. There were a couple of thousand people at the airport as we landed. A stewardess told me to please leave the plane last so the other passengers wouldn't be delayed, and while I waited, Jack Horrigan, the Bills' vice-president in charge of public relations, came in to welcome me. By the time we left the plane, everybody was chanting, "All the way with O.J." It was an exciting moment, especially because it took me by surprise. Then I glanced down at my striped casual slacks and gold sports shirt, and figured that I'd made my first mistake of the season. If they were going to greet me like this, the least I could have done was wear a coat and tie.

We arrived at the training camp at Niagara University about 11:00 P.M. Jack took me to the coaches' office first. Coach John Rauch spoke to me briefly and introduced me to the other coaches. Coach Rauch told me the schedule of practices—and added that they would have a big press conference for me the next day. My reaction to that was strange. It was practically the first time in my life that I felt bugged by attention from the press. I've always believed in cooperating with the press as completely as I can because the writers have been so good to me—and also because I like to help out anybody who's trying to do a good job. But here I was, feeling self-conscious and doubtful about what the coaches and players would think of me, and practically the first thing the coach has to tell me about is a press conference. For the next few days it was the same way. I was concerned with acting right and practicing well, and all I heard was that I had another meeting, interview, or picture-taking session in the next hour. I think I managed to hide my mood and act courteous, but I felt bugged by it all.

It was after bedcheck when I got to my dormitory room. Ben Gregory, my roommate, was asleep. He woke up and said, "How you doing, man," and we talked for a few minutes. A few other guys stopped by the door and just glanced in to see what I looked like. Max Anderson, the Bills' top running back the year before, stopped and said he was glad to meet me. Max turned out to be a great guy, and he showed his class that first night. I didn't realize it, but he had taken a lot of kidding—and some baiting from reporters—about how I would knock him out of his job. But he never showed me any bad feelings at all. The next morning, when I really wanted somebody to walk into breakfast with me, and Ben said he wanted to sleep late, Max and Haven Moses, the split end, went with me to help bear the brunt of the ribbing I knew I'd have to take.

Max, Haven, and I sat down at one breakfast table, and soon a bunch of the older guys came over to meet me. In a matter of minutes, old Tom Day took over the group. He called me Money Boy and The Black Savior, and he took my name, Orenthal, which is bad enough, and twisted it into Orentheus. It only took me a few days to learn what an unusual, warm man Tippy Day was; but I learned even more quickly that he was one of the team's elder statesmen, and he didn't let anybody get away with anything. During my first practice he started yelling at guys, "Okay, there's no contact, you can't tackle Orentheus—but you can hit him a little!" And after that practice he announced, "Line up right here, boys, O.J.'s taking loan applications."

My problems with my equipment weren't especially unusual, but the camp was so full of reporters and photographers that both my helmet and jersey threatened to become major sports issues. The helmet problem was simply that I've got a large, unusually shaped head; my hair also happened to be in as long a natural haircut as I've had in a long time. So there was no helmet around to fit me, and I went through my first few workouts bareheaded. One newspaper made up the headline, "O.J.'s not conceited, he's just got a big head." And Paul Maguire, the punter and the funniest guy on the Bills, said, "Who says Buffalo needs a new domed stadium? We can use the stadium we've got and just put O.J.'s helmet over it."

The jersey problem was a little more sensitive. A halfback named Gary McDermott had already been assigned Number 32, my old number at SC. Before I arrived, he had understandably told some people that he didn't want to give it up. And naturally he took some needling about it. Maguire told him he could have a new jersey—Number 32B. And Tippy Day said that McDermott could keep 32 unless I was willing to rent it from him for $300 a week. Anyway, at the first practice I looked for Gary and told him not to worry about it. He could keep 32 and I'd take 36. I wasn't going to let myself look like a prima donna over something as unimportant as that.

McDermott and Max Anderson were the first players to show me what professional football should be—the best side of it, that is. On that opening day for me, Coach Rauch's terminology was totally foreign. He would call something like a "half-right" and I'd have no idea where

I was supposed to go. He'd call a flare and it would be what I knew as a snake pattern at SC. But Gary and Max stood by me and told me what was going on. Here were two running backs that I was expected to deprive of a regular job—one of them even figured to get cut because of me—and they were going out of their way to help me.

After practice that first day, we all went over to the little Niagara Club, a kind of cafe on the campus. Maguire declared that the richest rookie would have to buy the beers for everybody. They also made me go through the traditional rookie initiation, singing my college fight song. I knew I'd have to go through that, so I had tried hard to get all the words straight in my mind, but I forgot them halfway and started to hum. All the guys booed and made me sit down. Overall, the evening was a lot of fun, and I got the impression that the older players were willing to accept me. After dinner I separated from the group and went to a special meeting with Coach Rauch. After missing a month of training, I was so far behind in learning my plays that he wanted to go over the entire system with me in a special session.

I was in a strange mood during those first few days in camp. Walking around the Niagara campus, I felt lost and uncomfortable. My teammates and coaches were cordial and helpful enough, but I couldn't shake the feeling that I was a latecomer and a kind of alien. I hate to feel dumb in any situation. Yet it seemed that I was constantly asking somebody when the next meeting started, where the coaches' offices were, or what the training camp routine was—and I couldn't help feeling out of things. Actually, I was overreacting to a lot of minor difficulties; I was no more lost than any other new face in camp. But I was going through a brand new experience, one that most athletes face when they first go away to a college. I had suddenly been transported from a world of familiar surroundings and people who considered me a hero into a strange environment full of men who were waiting for me to prove myself all over again. Moving smoothly from high school to San Francisco City College and then to USC, I had never faced such a sudden change in surroundings, so things struck me with the same force with which they might have hit a college freshman. I was preoccupied with the differences between California and Buffalo, between being a star and being a raw rookie—and between the overall attitudes of college and professional ballplayers.

Two years earlier, I had chosen to attend USC. I had known its people and its traditions, and had been welcomed by many friends. But as everyone knew, I sure hadn't chosen Buffalo. So I felt stupid when I had to ask for directions and favors, and doubtful about how long my welcome would last. I was anxious to find out just where my new friends would come from. In addition, I felt a definite change in my own attitude. I didn't feel that I was coming to play a game any more. It was more like reporting to a job. My previous football experience had been all glamour and excitement; from the moment practices began, everything had been rah-rah and football had seemed like the most important thing in the world. But sometime during the long summer, the contract battle, or the jolt of my arrival in camp, a boy's game had been turned into a man's job. I was beginning to work, not to play, at football.

My adjustment was made more difficult by the fact that I didn't have my mind completely focused on what I was doing. From the day I had been given a USC playbook, I had studied my assignments like mad. I had memorized them, talked about them, practically slept with them. But at Niagara, I took my playbook, looked it over—and then found some excuse to close it. I'd open a few letters, call Marguerite or Chuck, or find something else to think about. I just wasn't concentrating on football. On the surface I had plenty of enthusiasm, but I couldn't get myself to plunge into the game the way I should have. I went through several weeks in that state. I'd mess up a play and figure, "Well, I'll get it down soon." I'd get leg-weary in practice and say to myself, "Well, I'll get in top shape soon." Of course, I should have been spending extra hours studying the plays or running on my own after workouts—but I never did. I wasn't being intentionally careless or distracted, but I wasn't forcing myself to get going, either. I was suffering from a weird sensation that I had never known before. I just didn't feel like playing football. And I felt a little guilty about it.

As cluttered as my mind was with outside interests, I became pretty close to two of the younger Bills very quickly. One was my training camp roommate, Ben Gregory. The other was my roommate on the road, Robert James. You could hardly have found two people more different from one another.

Ben had just shaved his head when I arrived that first night. In the dim light of the dormitory room, the shaved part of his skull looked so much lighter than his face that he had a strange, almost ghostlike look—or maybe it just seemed that way because I felt so strange and scared myself on that first evening. Ben had a square, tough face with brows that were almost always creased in a look of concentration and determination. At a glance he looked like a mean man—but within minutes, he was smiling broadly and talking. In fact, he's hardly stopped talking since. He has got to be the most argumentative dude I've ever spent any time around.

Ben's background was quite similar to mine. He grew

up in a ghetto in Uniontown, Pennsylvania, became a high school football star just in time to keep him out of all kinds of possible trouble, and went on to an All-American career at the University of Nebraska. He was having a great rookie season in 1968, leading the Bills in rushing, until he tore up his knee in the sixth game of the season. When I met him, he was still hobbling, and as things turned out, he never did get back into uniform last year. He was, of course, a haunting example of just what can happen to any ballplayer. One week he was averaging 5.4 yards a carry, catching passes as well as any back in the league, and inspiring writers to call him one of the coming stars. Then he started to make a cut in a run against Miami—and it was all over. I was to see that sort of thing happen to a lot of my friends and teammates before the season ended. But seeing Ben gave me the first jolt. I'd hate to imagine what it would be like to sit out a season with an injury; I think I'd be impossible to live with, I'd be so stir-crazy. But Ben seemed to adjust to it pretty well.

Actually, Ben could probably handle almost any situation. He was married to a lovely white girl named Bonnie, and they had a son named Morgan. They met at Nebraska, and I imagined that interracial marriages weren't welcomed by the local white citizens there any more than they are at most predominantly white campuses. But I never heard Ben and Bonnie talk much about whatever difficulties they had faced. Knowing Ben, I assumed that he had just taken care of any problems that came up and then quietly forgotten about them. He had also adjusted to life in Buffalo better than most of the younger members of the Bills; he certainly accepted it more easily than I did. To make me feel at home, he even told me that we had a choice room in the campus dormitory. It was on the eighth floor and was supposed to have a superb view. I guess it did, if what you wanted to look at was Niagara University.

One reason that Ben never got flustered about major issues in his life was that he was always too busy debating about smaller ones. I think that three things made him so argumentative. First, he was so honest that he could never conceal his opinions or feelings on any subject; second, his inability to play football gave him a lot of nervous energy to work off; and third, he just loves to disagree. With our similar backgrounds, we naturally had similar views on many things—but you never would have known it from listening to us. A few days after I arrived, for example, somebody asked me about the election of Mayor Sam Yorty in Los Angeles. In a bitter and furious last-ditch attack on his black opponent, Thomas Bradley, Yorty had pulled out a narrow victory. I had been in L.A. during the campaign, and like everyone else in town, I had seen Yorty play up the racial issue to the fullest. I said so.

"How do you know that he won because of the racial issue?" said Ben. "I think you're wrong. You're just giving your opinion, and it's probably wrong."

I had admittedly been disappointed by the defeat of Bradley, a black moderate. But I wasn't expressing my political opinion, I was stating a fact. Anyone who listened to Yorty's speeches and read his campaign literature— whether they were for or against him—knew that race had been a crucial factor in his late surge. But Ben, who hadn't been anywhere near L.A. during the election, knew better, and it took me half an hour just to argue him to a draw. Then I heard a few days later that somebody else had told Ben that Yorty won *without* using the racial issue in the campaign—and Ben had argued for half an hour that he *had* used it. It was lucky that Ben was as smart as he was so he could keep coming up with enough facts to support any argument he felt like presenting.

After a few days with Ben, maybe I expected almost everybody to be ready for a discussion at any time. So the first time I settled down in a room with Robert James, I casually started a conversation. "I guess a lot of squad cuts are coming up in the next few weeks," I said. "The way I figure it, the guys most likely to go are . . ."

"I might be the next to go," he interrupted. "That's why I don't want to talk about it." That was Bob James's style. He came from Fisk, a small southern school not known for athletics, and signed as a free agent with little more than an outside hope of making the Bills. So he did very little but study his assignments, act respectful, and keep quiet. Later in the year I started kidding him about being *too* respectful, too ingrained with the deference that southern Negroes have always been trained to show toward white superiors. I knew he was naturally shy, and I didn't mean that he should become a wise guy or anything, but I did think that he should be more confident about expressing his feelings to people. He got mad a few times when I told him he was too country or too southern —but overall I think we both learned a lot from being around one another.

In those first weeks, though, I didn't kid Robert at all because I realized that he was going through a pretty terrifying period. Most observers could see that he was an exceptional young defensive back, a ferocious hitter with quick reactions—but he would have been the last to admit it. At Fisk, I understood that he had played just about every position—guard, linebacker, defensive back, or anything else that needed help. Because of the lack of competition, he had never been sure how good he might be. And when the coaches began shipping one guy after another into camp for tryouts, he became convinced that he would be lost in the shuffle. So after only a few weeks, he quietly packed up and left camp.

It turned out that he hadn't been overlooked at all. The coaches not only tracked him down and lured him back to camp, but they bought him contact lenses to improve his reaction to the ball. That made it obvious that they had high hopes for Robert, but it didn't take much of the pressure off him. I can't forget the night we lost to the Chicago Bears, 23-16, in the second game of the annual Cleveland exhibition doubleheader. I was pretty caught up in all the excitement that always surrounds that doubleheader, and I'd spent a lot of the day meeting guys on the other teams involved. Partly because I hadn't played too much—it had only been my third game after signing my contract—I still had a lot of adrenaline to burn, so I was talking more than I usually would have after a loss.

Bob was sitting on the edge of his bed when I came in, just staring down at the floor. Suddenly I remembered. He had been called on two straight pass interference penalties in the second half. One of them had looked to everyone like a bad call, but that wasn't much consolation to Bob. I quieted down and tried to cheer him up. He didn't respond very well, but I figured that it was better to be cheerful than to let him get even more depressed. "There's always next week," I said.

"The next cut's Tuesday," he mumbled. "I may not *have* a next week."

"Sure you will," I insisted, knowing that he didn't believe a word of it. We hadn't been able to use the locker room at the stadium, so I got ready to shower. "Come on," I told him, "take a good long shower and forget about it."

"I don't feel like showering," he said. "I don't feel like doing anything at all."

Slowly it sank into me. This was a feeling I had never

experienced before in football, but it was one that I would have to start understanding very quickly. The clichés about it only being a game are pretty shallow in any case, but when you've got a rich long-term contract and a bright future away from the sport, you can at least put the misfortunes of a given game in perspective. For the Robert Jameses in the Bills' camp, there was no perspective. Each game, each play, was a frightening moment that might change a whole career, a whole life. Robert James had devoted a grueling summer to training camp and his only pay had been his $100 check after each game. If he had been cut that night, he would have had $500 for five games, hardly enough to live on for those two months, much less to give him a financial cushion while he went back to school or looked for a job. If he made the team, on the other hand, he could look forward to decent salaries, publicity, and off-the-field jobs, a new way of life. Those were the stakes every time a pass was thrown in Robert's direction.

Suddenly I realized how unimportant all the talk about the "pressure" on me had been. Sure, there was pressure because I had a big contract and a big reputation, and I wanted to prove that I deserved both. That pressure might make headlines throughout the season. But the real pressure in pro football doesn't hit the O.J. Simpsons. It hits the Robert Jameses. As I was to learn very painfully throughout the educational days of training camp, it's that little-known pressure that makes pro ball one hell of a tough game.

Chapter Four

Generation Gap

In my first few days in camp, I was surprised to find that it was hard to tell the rookies from the veterans because even the most nervous fringe player would do his best to appear cool in front of the rest of the team. And as a matter of fact, many rookies had as much reason for coolness as the veterans. From the start, Coach Rauch made it clear that he was looking for youth, so if a veteran and a new player were about equal in a battle for a job, it figured that the younger man would get it. The competition for jobs was so wide-open that hardly anyone could really feel safe.

That situation made me start thinking about something that kept recurring to me throughout the season. On a team coming off a 1-12-1 season—a team struggling toward respectability and a future—everybody is a kind of rookie. Everybody is looking for his place, his special role in what he hopes will be a drive toward the top.

The Bills at the start of the 1969 season were a mysterious mixture of youth and age, strength and weakness. They still had remnants of the mighty defensive team that won American Football League titles in 1964 and

1965; yet they could not shake the fact that they had compiled the worst record in football in 1968. The Bills' story, in success as well as in failure, was not simply one of personnel. They had won championships because they had had great players; but they had also won because of a rare amount of cohesion and team feeling. They had finished last because of age and an incredible string of injuries; but again, there were those who felt that losing might have had something to do with attitude. I didn't know enough about the Bills to draw my own conclusions. But the events of my first few weeks gave me a much broader picture of what the Bills had been—and what they had a chance of becoming.

Most of the changes that shape pro football teams take place in swift, silent ways. A coach knocks softly on a door at seven in the morning and tells a player he has been cut; the man is gone before the rest of the guys wake up. A general manager makes a phone call; players and draft choices are shuffled back and forth, and a line of agate type in the paper lists the alterations in the lives of several people under the heading, "Football Transactions." In fact, the first time that I watched at close range while a player was cut, I hardly had a chance to think about what was happening.

There was a defensive lineman named Bill Wilkerson. Everybody just called him Wilkie. He had played college ball at Texas Western, then made the Bills' taxi squad in 1967, and missed 1968 with an injury. He was big— about 6'5" and 270 pounds—and seemed quick and aggressive. From what I later heard, I guess the coaches thought he made too many mistakes. I'm not sure what Wilkie himself thought, but I know one thing: He was totally convinced that he wouldn't make the team. In fact, when I first met him, he had already packed all his things. "I want to be ready," he said. "The coach will be here early tomorrow morning, and he'll want me to get going in a hurry. By the time you guys wake up, I'll be gone."

The day after he told me that, he was still around. Another day went by and I saw him again. It got to be almost a standing joke. Wilkie would say, "I'll be gone tomorrow," and the next day the guys would kid him and tell him to unpack his stuff.

The night after our game with Detroit, my first game, we went out to dinner—Wilkie, a defensive back named Henry King, and me. The restaurant owner saw me and gave me a bottle of champagne, and Wilkie had the predictable reaction: "Let's drink it to celebrate my leaving."

"Wilkie, you're not leaving," I told him. "I'll save this until you do leave—and let's hope we'll never have to drink it."

The next day he stuck his head into my room and said, "Let's open that champagne. I'll be leaving tonight." I laughed and said, "You won't get cut." He shook his head and tried to laugh, too, and I looked into his face and felt how fiercely he was hoping that I was right. I was really beginning to like Wilkie. I hoped that I was right, too. And I was glad when he changed the subject.

"If I ever come to L.A.," he said, "you'd better not act like you don't know me."

"I'm just worried that if I come to that little town you're from, you'll act like you don't know me." And so our routine went on. Then, after a few more days, Wilkie came in and told me to open the champagne, and as much as I wanted to keep joking about it, I could see by his face that this time he meant it. He had been cut. He was trying very hard to act like it didn't bother him, but he wasn't doing a very good job. Henry King came in behind him and nodded to me; it was true. "All right," I said, "let's open that champagne."

But Wilkie didn't seem very interested in it anymore, and I just held the bottle in my hands while we talked about nothing for a few minutes. I wondered what the right thing was to say, and realized that there is no right thing; while I was still considering it, Wilkie just turned around and walked out. I thought he would come back when he got himself together, but he never did. Wilkie was gone. He never did drink that champagne. And we never heard from Wilkie again.

That, I guess, is the way it usually happens. But on a team going through the adjustment to a new coach and a youth movement, it didn't always happen that quietly. The second week I was in camp, Coach Rauch cut three veterans. One was Tom Janik, a twenty-nine-year-old strong safety who had been hurt the year before and lost his job to John Pitts. He was soon picked up by the Boston Patriots as a punter. The second was Eddie Rutkowski, the courageous all-around player who had wound up playing quarterback the year before, after all the regular quarterbacks were crippled. Eddie had lasted for six years with Buffalo largely on hustle. He was a receiver, a safety, a punt returner, and a running back—and when asked to fill in, he willingly accepted the quarterback spot although he had not played the position since college. His performance had made him the Bills' Most Valuable Player in 1968. He was certainly one of the most popular Bills, with both the fans and the players. The decision to let him go was undoubtedly understandable to the experts, but it aroused a lot of emotion in Buffalo. He wound up in Montreal, doing his thing by filling in at almost every position for the Alouettes in the Canadian League.

The third cut of the week was George Flint, a guard who had been a part of the Bills' championship teams.

Weighing only about 240 pounds, Flint had never really been heavy and strong enough to be a star lineman, but he had been a part of those unusually closeknit Buffalo teams of 1964 and 1965, and was very popular with the older guys. Flint had played briefly for Rauch in Oakland a year before, and the coach had reportedly talked him out of a possible retirement to bring him to camp. Flint was supposed to have had a good business in Arizona, but when Rauch called him, he placed the whole thing in somebody else's hands and came back; he just couldn't turn down a chance to get back into football.

He was one of the hardest-working players in camp, and a lot of the veterans were hoping he would hang on. But, according to some of the guys, the coach called him in and said, "You're doing a great job, the best job I've seen you do either in Oakland or here. But we've got to make room for the younger guys." The veterans were pretty upset by that comment. "If you're going to cut a man," one of them told me, "you shouldn't tell him what a hell of a job he's doing. Just say 'we're going to youth,' and leave it at that."

Not many of us knew about Flint's being cut until late that night when all hell broke loose in the dormitory. A lot of the older Bills—the ones from those championship teams—were really raising hell in the hallways. Tom Sestak, Tom Day, Ron McDole, Paul Maguire—they had been through the best and the worst years together, and now they had obviously given their friend Flint a wild sendoff. They were really blowing off some steam. They knocked the lights out. They threw some chairs around. They started smashing the ashtrays onto the floor—and those ashtrays had been bolted into the walls.

At first it was just a crazy, loud scene. Then I looked at those guys and it started to get to me. These were grown men who had at one time reached the top of their profession. They had reached it as a group, and now they were watching that group dissolve. My generation is built around protests; we've all learned to speak out and express ourselves on almost anything. But that night I realized that I was watching another generation protesting —and those guys seemed like much more than a bunch of men who'd been drinking to lament the cutting of a friend. They had raised hell, on and off the football field, through a glorious era of the Buffalo Bills; if that era had to end, they would protest it with a little more hell-raising.

I walked out into the hall and saw Tippy Day. "Is this all happening," I asked him, "because they cut Flint?"

He stopped yelling and looked straight at me. "You'll be here long enough," he said softly, "and then you'll understand it."

Tippy started tearing things up again, running up and down the hall with the other guys, and I went into Haven Moses's room and sat down with Haven and Max Anderson. In a few minutes, Maguire came through the door. Knowing Maguire, I naturally expected a lot of jokes and horsing around, especially since they'd all been drinking all night. But Maguire sat down and began talking very emotionally: "You guys don't understand now. But there was a love on this team. You can't feel it yet, but you will when you've been in pro ball for a few years. When forty guys are working together for something—and when they achieve it the way we did for a few years— they get a very special feeling. It sounds corny when you talk about it, but you can only call it love."

It was a pretty sentimental moment because of all people, Maguire seemed the least likely to talk to us like that. Maguire jokes around during practices, meetings, even during losing games. I would have thought he could laugh at anything. And here he was, sitting across from

us and talking about George Flint, whom I had barely
known, and making us feel almost as bad as he did. "This
was a friend," he said. "This was a member of a team.
George has a business to go back to and he won't starve
or anything, but that doesn't make it any easier to realize
that you're never going to play with him again. When
a guy's time comes, it comes—and you can't escape the
fact that he's through. It makes it a cruel game."

"That's why I've made the comment that I'd like to
have five good years and quit while I'm on top," I told him.

"You won't quit," Maguire said. "You'll play more than
five years. Why do you think a guy like Johnny Unitas is
playing? What about Joe Namath, with all that money
and those bad knees? Or Bill Mathis of the Jets, with all
the money he's made in stocks? They've got money, but
they love the game. You'll feel the same way. Five years,
O.J.? Hell, this gets into your blood."

Maguire went down the hall, and I went back to my
own room and started talking to Ben Gregory about what
he had said. Then Tippy Day came in—sounding just as
emotional as Maguire. "You think you had spirit at USC,"
he told me, "but wait until you play with these guys for
a few years. At USC, you finally break up and go on to
bigger and better things. When you finish up here, you
don't go on in football. You're just starting your career,
but you'll see." Tippy was getting pretty choked up. "You'll
see," he repeated. "You just have to stick around awhile,
like we have. We've all got about one or two years left, so
seeing a friend get cut means a lot. We all know that our
day is coming soon."

Tom Sestak's day came the next morning. Sestak had
been one of the best linemen in AFL history; pictures of
him slashing in on a quarterback, with his arms raised
high in a patented gesture, were practically symbols of
the league for several seasons. I grew up in NFL terri-

tory and there were years when I probably couldn't have named a half-dozen AFL linemen—but Sestak would have been one of them. A big, quiet man who never let up, he had been one of the leaders of the greatest defensive clubs in AFL history. In fact, Sestak, McDole, Day, and Jim Dunaway had been the front four on the only AFL club to score a shutout in a title game. The 1965 Bills had smothered the favored San Diego Chargers, 23-0, as the linemen never gave John Hadl a safe moment.

But knee operations had slowed Sestak for several seasons, and a second-year man named Bob Tatarek had been getting most of the playing time in camp. We had all figured that Sestak would be going—and he must have known it too. He knew that he had been placed on waivers and offered in trades, and he knew that everyone had turned him down because of his knees. In fact, he must have talked to the coaches on the day Flint was cut, and they had undoubtedly told him that he might as well retire. In other words, he knew his time was up that night.

Yet he stayed with the team. I would have expected a guy who knew he was through to raise hell with his friend Flint, and then go out on the town. In fact, Sestak and Maguire had their own bar in Buffalo and they had countless friends in town; Tom could easily have had a lot of action far away from that boring dormitory. Almost everybody else was dying to get away from that place out in the boondocks—and here was Sestak coming back to spend a final night there. That helped me understand why they were raising so much hell. These were men who wanted to stay together. They wanted to remain a team. These were the Bills of 1965, the Bills who had won everything. And it was all over.

But one big question remained: If the old Bills were fading away, where were the new Bills who were supposed to start a bright new era? Naturally I hoped I was one of them; I guess most of the young guys in camp felt the same way. But the old Bills had so much more than mere talent. Even if we had a lot of talent, where were we going to find those extra factors that made champions of the old Bills? We still needed experience, pride, and cohesiveness—and we spent the whole season searching for those elements. Most important, we needed a leader. And I'm not sure we ever found one.

The most obvious candidates were the offensive and defensive captains, Jack Kemp and Harry Jacobs. Kemp had many leadership credentials. He was president of the AFL Players Association, he had directed the Bills to two league championships, and he was an articulate, highly respected veteran. But he was hurt during those first confused weeks of training camp, and even when he was available, Coach Rauch tended to use rookie James Harris and substitute Tom Flores at quarterback. The coach didn't seem likely to stake the Bills' future on a thirty-four-year-old quarterback—especially one like Kemp, who had a reputation for having a strong mind of his own when it came to following coaches' instructions.

On defense, middle linebacker Jacobs was an established leader. An active member of the Fellowship of Christian Athletes, he loved to give speeches and pep talks. But the defense was still a veteran unit, working on its own to maintain its pride and rating as one of the best in football. On offense, we had little direct contact with Jacobs; we needed a leader of our own. Of all the veterans, the one who impressed me most quickly as being a genuine leader was Billy Shaw, the incredibly hard-working All-Pro guard. Just by his example, Billy provided a lot of spirit. But it still seemed awfully hard for one offensive lineman to take charge of the team, and Billy definitely wasn't given to pep talks. I gradually became more and more convinced that the answer to our leader-ship problems would have to come from one of us younger men.

The Bills were suffering from an unusual identity crisis. We fell into two distinct and diverse groups—the veterans and the young players—and sometimes it was hard to tell whether we were fading or rebuilding, aging or youthful. We needed something or somebody to pull us all together and show us once and for all what kind of team we were. A big game or a big play might have done it; one player or one group might also have done it. I might have been able to do it myself, with a little more effort or boldness or luck. But in camp it seemed much too early to think in such terms. As people kept reminding me, I was just a rich rookie.

Chapter Five

The Learning Process

On my first night in camp, I lost some money in a friendly card game. Maybe a few of the guys thought they had a pigeon with a big bankroll, but I straightened them out pretty quickly. I didn't have many losing nights after that. I love to play cards, and there were plenty of opportunities on the Bills, as there are on most professional athletic teams. The younger guys played a lot of games; the older ones preferred to stick to poker—and I took my chances with both groups. After that initial setback, I handled the cards pretty well. I only wish I had been able to adjust as quickly to the other challenges I had to face.

From the moment I was drafted, I had listened to endless speculation about how I would adapt myself to a new coach, a new system, and new competition. In all honesty, I hadn't paid much attention to the talk; maybe I should have taken it more seriously. Ever since high school, I had enjoyed the feeling that if I worked hard enough and ran with the ball enough, I'd get my yardage and my touchdowns. But it turned out that I fell short of both conditions. I didn't work as hard as I should have, and sometimes it seemed that I would never get my hands on the ball again.

There are no simple explanations for the way things worked out. I spent a good part of the season trying to figure out just what was happening, and I'm not sure I ever found all the answers. But one thing was clear. In terms of football as well as atmosphere, southern California and Buffalo were as different as day and night—and I spent months just trying to grope my way through the Buffalo scene and the Buffalo system.

The most striking contrast between college and pro ball was between the head coaches. USC coach John Mc-Kay was dapper and witty, always breaking up meetings or press conferences with wry jokes. He was the kind of man who could make you feel close to him without using a lot of speeches; just a few words from him could let you know what you had to do—and also make you want to do it. He also leaned heavily on his assistants. When it was time for some really fiery pep talks, coach Marv Goux would take over. When someone needed instruction, he would get it from an assistant, with Coach McKay making a few suggestions.

Coach Rauch presented an altogether different appearance. He seldom wore the hats or sharp jackets that distinguished John McKay; in his windbreaker on the sidelines, he really looked more like an assistant coach at a glance. And he took a much more direct part in practices than Coach McKay. Everyone knew, of course, that Rauch had left the Oakland Raiders after some strong disagreements with Al Davis, the managing general partner. And it was no secret that there were two schools of thought on the Raiders' great success. One said that Rauch had done very well despite constant interference from Davis; the other said that Davis had really built the team and was in charge, and Rauch was little more than a puppet.

Nobody in Buffalo seriously believed the second theory, but the fact remained that Rauch was totally in charge of a team for the first time—and he wanted to assert virtually complete control. So he surrounded himself with an unusually young band of assistants, right down to Bugsy Engelberg, a small, round twenty-three-year-old "kicking coach" who came from Oakland and seemed to be more of a mascot than a teacher.

Coach Rauch himself was the backfield coach, so I received a lot more direct attention from him than I had from other coaches. "The offense will be difficult for you to master," he told me. "It's easy for me, but I've read the book six times." I wish I'd read the book more thoroughly; I might have avoided some of my early problems.

Technically, my first weakness came on what we called flare action passes. Coach Rauch planned to use me often as a receiver, hoping to isolate me one-on-one on a linebacker so I could break free for some long passes. I knew that this play had been a feature of the Oakland offense, and it certainly seemed like a logical way to score some quick points. But all those X's and O's on the blackboard that showed me sailing away from helpless linebackers weren't quite so simple when that linebacker was trying to tie me up. On most of our flare patterns, my duty was to block the linebacker if he rushed toward the passer— and to run my pattern if the linebacker didn't rush. But unfortunately, we weren't the only ones who knew that a linebacker couldn't cover me in the open field; the linebackers knew it, too, so they did everything possible to slow me down.

I heard Coach Rauch's voice again and again in those early weeks: "Damn it, O.J., you *can't* let that guy tie you up. They're rushing our passer, so you've *got* to get free quickly. *Drive* on that backer. Get him going the way you want him to go, and then fake somewhere else. O.J., no linebacker should be able to stay with you. You should be able to beat anyone."

I should have, but very often I didn't—and it bothered me almost as much as it bothered the coach. A number of times, I made simple mental mistakes, going in the wrong direction and blowing chances to shake free. Other times I just got chopped down—and a few times I just didn't run my patterns as enthusiastically as I should have because I knew I wouldn't be getting the ball on the play. In most of the cases, I had to blame myself.

But if I was a slow learner, it wasn't because I wasn't smart enough to learn a system and it wasn't because I didn't want to learn. The problem, I think, was that I was being asked to become a very different kind of ballplayer. At USC I carried the ball thirty or forty times a game and caught a few passes as a change of pace. Coach Rauch wanted me to become more balanced, as good a receiver as I was a runner. It made sense because his system tries to offer a lot of varied weapons. But in those first few weeks, I couldn't help being a little discouraged, not only about my lack of progress as a receiver, but also about my running.

I felt that I was stutter-stepping instead of hitting the holes crisply, and I seemed to lack the instant burst of speed that had allowed me to break out of pileups and sprint for big gains in college. My holdout was partly responsible; I was still far short of top shape. But I was confident that I could recover my timing and quickness as I ran with the ball more and more often.

Unfortunately, that didn't happen. Even in practice, I seemed to spend more time running pass patterns than I did running from scrimmage. Again, I understood the coach's reasoning and respected what he was trying to do. But personally, it was frustrating to feel that I wasn't accomplishing everything I felt capable of. After a few weeks I thought about approaching the coach about it. I wanted to say something like, "I'd really like to run the ball more in practice so I can sharpen up and run better in games." But I was afraid that it would come out sounding like, "I'm O.J. Simpson, the big star. You've got to let me run the ball." So I never did bring it up. I just kept hoping.

Another thing that struck me about pro coaching was the lack of emotion involved. At USC, there was a very tense, almost constant emotional charge in the air. If a coach yelled or cursed at us, the whole team would freeze and seem to say, "We'd better get it right this time." I don't think it's exaggerating to call the reaction genuine fear. In the pros, if a coach gets mad, the team's response will still be, "Let's get it right this time"—but it will be a more businesslike approach. Players will try to get it right because they know it is part of their job, not because they're scared.

In college, we were trying to psyche ourselves, get ourselves up to outhit the other guys on every play. With the Bills, I guess it was just expected that you'd be up for every play, so there was little psyching, little rah-rah. At half time, for example, the SC dressing room would be wild. Coach McKay would give a fight talk, and then Coach Goux would take over and really go at it—and we'd go out for the second half ready to tear somebody apart. With Coach Rauch, half times were for sound technical discussions, to make adjustments and corrections. I was sure that was the professional approach, the best way to accomplish things in pro ball. But in those first few weeks, sometimes I couldn't help feeling that things were a little flat. A few times I wished I could hear one more of old Marv Goux's speeches, just to make me feel like really playing football again.

The Bills had played two games before I reported to camp, a loss to the Houston Oilers and a victory over the

Washington Redskins. I began practicing the week before the Detroit Lions game, but I didn't expect to play much in that one. I had just been feeling my way, listening to Max Anderson and Gary McDermott and trying to run in the general direction of where I was supposed to go. When we took off for the Saturday night game in Detroit, I was undoubtedly as unprepared as I've ever been for a game. Physically, I was far from good condition; mentally, I was preoccupied with many things outside football. But I wasn't even keyed up enough to worry. I felt loose and re-laxed, and the trip seemed more like a brief vacation than a football game.

My first thought when we reached Detroit the night before the game was to contact my good friend Earl McCullouch. Earl and I had played together in football and track, and he had graduated from SC a year ahead of me and became the NFL Rookie of the Year for the Lions. Earl is the best high hurdler and wide receiver I know, and one of the worst horseplayers and poker players. As usual, I was looking forward to finding out about the latest debts he had piled up. I couldn't reach him that night, however, and just went out for a while with Tippy Day and a few other players.

The next morning I was delighted to get a message from Wilson Bowie, who had played behind me at USC. Somebody came into our team meeting as it ended and told me that Wilson was outside, and Tippy and I went out to see him. He was waiting in a car, with his knee in a cast—and it occurred to me that he was one of the un-luckiest athletes around. Wilson had always been a promising back. But in his first year at SC, he played behind Mike Garrett. The next fall he was slated to start, but hurt his knee and lost his spot to Don McCall, who's also made it in the pros now. Then his knee was still giving him trouble when I arrived, and he played behind me for two years. In four years he was behind two Heisman Trophy winners and another running back who wound up as a pro. The Lions still took a chance on him in a late round of the draft, and I understood that he was doing very well until he injured his knee again. It must have been a hell of a blow to him, and I knew that he'd be feeling very low.

So when I saw him, I laughed at him and yelled, "Someone really kicked your tail. It's just as well, you sucker, because if you'd been playing tonight, I'd have broken it for you myself." This is an SC tradition. I don't know what crazy source it stems from, but when a guy gets hurt at SC, you never act sympathetic; you laugh and kid him—and make him laugh with you. We've all gotten the same treatment—me, Earl, Mike Taylor, Bubba Scott, anybody—and I think it says something about the entire USC approach to football. We're all proud and happy to be Trojans, and we learn very quickly that we're not going to let any setbacks get us down too much. Anybody who saw us after the few games we lost knows that no sulking goes on in an SC locker room. To an outsider, though, I'll admit that it's a little hard to explain. Tippy Day looked at us as if we were nuts, as I stood there laughing at Wilson's cast—and Wilson leaned out of the car window and laughed just as enthusiastically.

Later Tippy and I had lunch with Earl and Mel Farr, a Lion running back who played college football at UCLA. Since I'd seen The Pearl only a month earlier in L.A., we didn't exchange any earth-shattering news. He hadn't gotten out of debt, or anything as drastic as that, since I'd left him at Hollywood Park Racetrack. After we ate, Earl dropped me back at the hotel so I could rest up—for a game I didn't really expect to play in.

On the bench that night, I couldn't believe how loose everybody seemed. Maguire was cracking jokes and other guys were laughing and kidding around. Even though it was an exhibition game, I hadn't expected things to be this calm. "This is really something," I said to Maguire. "You seem so relaxed."

"Shut up and get over here, kid," he snapped back. "Stand next to me so all the photographers will get me in those pictures, too."

The first quarter was a weird experience, sitting on the bench and watching other guys move the ball on offense. The photographers stayed clustered around me and a few of the guys kept kidding me; then I received a jolt. "O.J.," called Coach Rauch. "Go in and run a ninety-four with a seven-corner flare action."

By the time I reached the huddle and spoke to quarterback Tom Flores, I could hardly remember the play number—much less what I was supposed to do on that play. We were on the Detroit twenty, and the play called for me to run a pass pattern into the right corner of the end zone. I ran it well—I sure had enough nervous energy bottled up inside me—and I was wide-open. But Haven Moses was just as free, and Tom threw to him for the touchdown. I had a very minor part in it, but it was still a sweet feeling.

I stayed in for only one play in the second period, and then I played the whole fourth quarter. The writers were naturally dissecting every move I made, and the official figures later showed that I was in for a total of nineteen plays. I ran four times for 19 yards and caught a pass—a pretty good catch, I thought—from James Harris for 38 yards. But to me the game didn't seem to break down into neat statistics. The first time I ran, it was a trap up the middle and I got stopped for no gain; the next time, I ran a sweep for 14 yards. But both plays seemed to run together in my mind. I just knew that I was watching guys block and hit, and I was getting tackled, and I thought,

"This isn't as physical as I expected. It isn't that much different from getting hit in college." I don't know exactly what I had anticipated, but I guess I had an idea that pro tacklers would really try to destroy you. That night altered my conception of that—at least until a few months later when I first ran into Bobby Bell of the Chiefs.

I was excited about the showing of James Harris that night. James, who's from Grambling, was operating under as many pressures as any quarterback could ask for: He was a rookie, he was still trying to learn a new system and gain confidence, and he was black. I was rooting for him to make it as the first really successful black quarterback in pro ball, and he had a good night, completing seven of thirteen passes and having a few others dropped.

The player who made the strongest impression on me, however, was Billy Shaw. After my first run, he came back into the huddle talking to the other linemen, saying, "Come on, boys, come on. We've got to block for him." I hadn't sat down and analyzed what to expect from various veterans, but if I had, I don't think I would have guessed right on Billy Shaw. He was a nine-year veteran, a perennial All-Pro and a white native of Mississippi; I don't think many people would have predicted that he would knock himself out for a publicized black rookie making several times his own salary. But those people wouldn't have known the special feeling that Billy and a lot of the other older Bills shared. Going into that game, I would have been a little scared to even approach Billy Shaw, a man who had accomplished so much more in pro ball than I had. But he talked to me and encouraged me from the start. From that point on, I think that Billy and I shared as strong a mutual respect as any men on the team—and that makes me as proud as almost anything else that happened during the season.

Working with Billy, I got a true feeling of what it meant

to be a professional. In an early practice, I ran a sweep that I felt was going a little too wide. On the way back to the huddle, I said to him, "Couldn't we turn that play up field a little sooner?"

As soon as I said it, I was sorry. "Here you're hardly playing," I said to myself, "and you're trying to tell Billy Shaw what to do."

But Billy answered, "We can try it and see," and I knew that he understood my feelings. I didn't want to be the boss or give orders; I wanted to make every play work as well as possible. And so did he—as I saw throughout the year.

I was fairly pleased with the first game, even though we lost, 24-12. I had enjoyed some good moments on the field, and I had spent my time on the bench trying to recognize all our formations and plays so I'd be further along in my knowledge of the system. I was also flattered when Coach Rauch was quoted as saying, "I hadn't planned to use O.J. as much as I did, but he gave me confidence that he knew his plays." Reporters crowded around me after the game, and it felt good to be in the midst of some action after holding out for so long and wondering when I'd finally return. It was only when I returned to the hotel that I realized that something was vaguely wrong. For the first time in my life, I'd been through an entire football game and I wasn't even tired.

During the next week, my first full one with the Bills, I really started to feel like part of the group. In fact, the veterans—Maguire, Tippy, Billy Shaw, and Paul Costa—changed my nickname from O.J. to J.O., meaning Jack-Off, because I got away with several crazy jokes on them. One night I walked into a room where Joe O'Donnell, Tom Janik, and Costa were playing cards. "Did you hear about the big trade?" I asked. "The Jets traded Don Maynard and Emerson Boozer to San Diego for Lance Alworth." They started spreading the word around, and everybody was talking about the trade before Billy Shaw came in, laughing at them, and telling them I had made it up. That's when Maguire gave me the name J.O.

Later I told Paul Costa that the coach was looking for him. I said it was about something to do with the Selective Service. Paul, who is one of the most powerful-looking men I've ever met, was twenty-seven at the time and he shouldn't have had any draft worries. But I must have been pretty convincing. "The coach was saying, 'They can't do that to Paul,'" I went on—and Paul really got upset. But Joe O'Donnell was with us and interrupted: "Don't worry, J.O.'s lying again."

"How can you tell," I asked. "I think I lie pretty effectively."

"You do," Joe said. "Except that when you lie you look so serious and intent on what you're saying, it gives you away. When you're saying something and you're laughing, that's the only time I can tell you're telling the truth." I figured that it was something to keep in mind for my acting career.

We played the Baltimore Colts in Buffalo's War Memorial Stadium that week. Before the game, the guys kidded me a lot about making my debut in that stadium. The drab old structure was certainly a contrast to the Los Angeles Coliseum, where I'd spent my college career, and they joked that maybe I would refuse to play until Buffalo built itself a new stadium. Personally, I was pretty preoccupied with my own role, wondering just how much I'd absorbed in a week of practice. Then I walked out onto the field for the warmups and saw the mass of white and blue uniforms at the other end, and all other thoughts were shoved out of my mind by the realization: "These are the Baltimore Colts."

I was in awe. In my high school and junior college days, the Colts had stood for the best football in the world. I remembered thinking that Gino Marchetti, Big Daddy Lipscomb, Lenny Moore, and Johnny Unitas had to be the greatest players that ever lived. The Green Bay Packers had come along to dominate the game after the Colts, and the Jets had whipped Baltimore in the Super Bowl, but those early memories all flooded back when I saw the Colts that night. It was the first thing about playing pro ball that I couldn't take in stride: I was actually going to play a game against John Unitas.

The Colts beat us, 20-7, in a way that dramatized the difference between experience and youth. I didn't feel that they were superior physically, but they won with the kind of finesse I would have to get used to in pro competition. Unitas, who replaced Earl Morrall late in the first half, wasn't overwhelming; but he made good on five of eight third-down plays and threw one 70-yard bomb for a touchdown. They were the kind of big plays a good team makes —the kind that we would keep looking for all season.

Defensively, their blitzes and stunts confused us fairly often, and they got to our quarterbacks seven times. I missed a few assignments, and I got rapped with my hardest shot yet when blitzing linebacker Sidney Williams caught me in the head with his forearm. I also got called for holding once, but overall I thought my performance showed a slight improvement. On at least two runs, I was able to make quick cuts and squirm loose to turn short gains into longer ones, and I wound up with 25 yards in five carries. I felt that my timing and my quickness were slowly returning, but I also felt that they'd return a lot sooner if I ran the ball more. But it was still the preseason schedule, and the whole bright year lay ahead, so I wasn't too worried about anything.

There was something unusually festive about our pre-season game against the Chicago Bears in Cleveland; that huge Cleveland crowd—more than 85,000—gives special impact to any event. We were matched against the Bears in the first game of the doubleheader, with the Browns facing Green Bay in the second. Our game was billed as a confrontation between Gale Sayers and me, and I guess the fact that we did draw so much attention verified one of our claims during contract negotiations—that the Bills would become a much bigger preseason attraction with my name, and make a lot more money.

The Packers were staying at the same hotel we used, and when we arrived the night before the game, I had a chance to meet a lot of the stars I'd watched on television for years. I spent some time with Herb Adderly and Marv Fleming, and had some long talks with middle linebacker Ray Nitschke and Jerry Kramer, the guard who had re-tired after the previous season. Jerry, whose first book, *Instant Replay*, was such a success, told me that he was working on another book, about incentive and motivation. He said that he had asked a lot of athletes, "What makes you want to keep competing?" It was a question I'd con-sidered many times myself, and I was interested to find that Jerry and I shared many conclusions about it. We agreed that money wasn't the main thing. Just as Maguire had said on the night Flint was cut, there are an awful lot of men who stay in football long after money doesn't matter much to them. And some of the greatest athletes, such as Sayers and Leroy Kelly, seem to get even hungrier as the years go by and their salaries increase. I've always had a drive within me, a hunger that probably was born

in the ghetto. I fought, stole, hustled, got into trouble—
and I came within inches of blowing my chances to become somebody. But I always had that drive to become the
best at whatever I did, and with the help of some luck at
the right times, it kept me going toward the top. Jerry
talked about the letdown the Packers had suffered the previous season after Vince Lombardi left them. He said that
they had gotten a little spoiled, a little too dependent on
Vince for their inspiration; when they suddenly had to
reach down and motivate themselves, they didn't always
manage to do it. I thought that maybe I was fortunate in
that sense; I'd never needed some outside source to supply
my incentive.

I had a conversation with Nitschke that, in retrospect,
struck me as very ironic. Nitschke has a very smooth, hip
way of talking and he kept warning me, "Check that
Butkus, baby. You've got to watch him all the time. When
you go through there, don't get too close to Butkus because
he'll clothesline you in a minute."

Of course, I knew that Dick Butkus was football's best
linebacker, and I knew that he was a guy who went all out
every minute—and sometimes kept going all out after the
whistle blew. I had heard him called a cheap-shot artist,
and I had heard other people say that he just put out 110
percent. Personally, I'd seen him take a few shots that I
thought were cheap, but he wasn't one of those guys who
just went around looking for chances to take shots. He
played so intensely on every play that sometimes he did
hit late or illegally, but he was trying so hard that you had
to figure him as just a 110 percent ballplayer. The funny
thing was that this warning about him was coming from
Nitschke, the man some people call the dirtiest linebacker
of all time. When Ray was telling me what Butkus would
do, he was really thinking about what he would have liked
to do to me himself. "Don't get near Butkus," he said.

"He'll get you somehow or other." And I smiled and thought that whatever Butkus managed to do to me, he had undoubtedly learned from Nitschke.

Anyway, Nitschke undoubtedly got to me, because when the game started I was on the bench, looking especially for Butkus. Just from watching him on films all week, I knew he was a maniac—and what Nitschke had said made me all the more aware of him. But he didn't play too much in the first half, and when I went in for the first time in the second quarter, I was relieved to find him out of the lineup. Everything started off very well for me. I ran a couple of traps, then caught two screen passes for 23 yards. I also returned two kickoffs for 60 yards and—my best moment—I threw the key block on Bubba Thornton's 97-yard touchdown return.

It was not a game that will be long remembered in football history, and the big battle between Gale and me didn't produce any records. He made 12 yards; I made 8. In fact, one of the few outstanding plays was made by Paul Maguire, who was one of the game's best punters as well as the team comedian. He got a low pass from center once, fumbled it around, got chased by half the Bear team—and finally managed to make a good kick with five guys on top of him. He got up slowly, walked to the sideline, took his helmet off, and glared at the nearest photographer. "Did you get some good shots of that kick?"

The photographer didn't look like he had even noticed the kick, but he said, "Oh yeah, sure, buddy."

"Good," said Maguire. "Send me three of each Monday morning."

When the photographer, probably feeling guilty, started taking pictures of Maguire like mad, Paul called to me. "Hey O.J., come over here and pose with me. You poor kid, nobody ever wants to take your picture."

That night, nobody should have taken my picture. It

was my worst game of the exhibition season. After a pretty good start, I messed up a couple of assignments and lined up on the wrong side of the formation once. And I never did feel that I was running well. Again, I would have given anything for more work. But I was only supposed to play the second and fourth periods, and in those periods it seemed as if the Bears always had the ball. So I carried exactly three times.

After my second play, I was hit with a realization that stunned me. I felt lazy, slow, unprepared for a lot of action. I guess I was too accustomed to USC football, where I was in on so many plays that I was totally wrapped up in the action; there, I never had time to think about staying alert or in shape. But with the Bills, I wasn't doing enough in the games; and I hadn't made up for that lack of work with extra effort in practice. I felt tired, a little leg-weary—and I said to myself, "You sucker, you should have stayed out after practice and run some laps."

In the last quarter I was running a pass pattern, and James Harris had to scramble out of the pocket. Seeing James in trouble, I turned back toward him, racing across the middle. And for the first time, I knew what it meant to hear footsteps. Throughout my football life, I've felt proud of the fact that I would go after the ball no matter what happened, and I didn't care who was trying to hit me. But as I cut across the middle, I suddenly thought, "Butkus is in the game now. Where is he?" The ball was thrown toward me, but a little behind me. I tried to turn and catch it, but I couldn't do it. As the ball flew by, someone hit me. It wasn't Butkus. But as I went back to the huddle, I was laughing at myself; I had really let the whole Butkus idea psyche me out.

After the game, I didn't feel too badly; it was only after I watched the films that I saw a lot of my mistakes. But a few little things kept going through my mind. One was that play when I heard Butkus's footsteps; another was my first kickoff return. It was a "middle" return, and as I got going I saw a lot of guys dropping ahead of me. So at about the twenty-five-yard-line, I hurdled two guys and landed on another one. I could have escaped the third guy; he was grabbing me but he was down and didn't have a good angle. Another tackler was coming from across the field, but I was pretty sure I could beat him, too. So I dug in and got ready to take off—and that burst of speed just didn't come. I tried to stiff-arm the tackler, but he ran right through my arm and nailed me. At that point, I saw very clearly just how much work lay ahead for me. And time was running out. In two weeks, the regular season would be starting.

Chapter Six

The Toughest Lesson

Two weeks to go: The pace of my workouts, my private life, and my jumbled thoughts picked up. Up to that point, things had been tentative and exploratory. Small matters might have pleased or annoyed me; I might have searched for hints of what the season would be like. Now I wanted to start thinking in broader terms; my mood was expansive and optimistic. The excitement of the season was beginning to get to me.

Events piled up ahead. There would be a homecoming in Los Angeles, a final exhibition game against the Rams in the Coliseum where I had enjoyed my best USC moments. There would be many mundane tasks in Buffalo, including getting our new apartment into decent shape before Marguerite and Arnelle arrived the next week. And there would be the fascination of watching the young Buffalo team take shape before the opening game—and establishing my place on that team.

On the Sunday night after the Bear game, I had a nightmare; it was one of those dreams that I couldn't recall too vividly when I woke up, but I had a vague feeling that I had died or something. I figured that it had something to do with my preoccupations about the coming day. I knew that we would be watching the game films, and the Bear game had been a terrible one for me. Ben Gregory had stayed downtown that night, so I had to drive in alone to the stadium from our apartment building, which was in a suburb called Amhurst. As usual, I got lost. When you're used to the well-marked freeways of southern California, Buffalo is an easy place to get lost in; every time you think you have one gray, nondescript street straight in your mind, you find out that there are a million others just as gray and nondescript. As I drove around, I began to get scared that I'd be late for the meeting, which would have been really embarrassing. I finally did get there on time, but I was feeling low.

The game that had seemed bad in person looked even worse on the movie screen. On the way out of the session, I told several guys that it had been the worst performance of my career. I didn't get any arguments; I guess they were at least hoping that I wouldn't get any worse than that. When we trotted onto the field in our sweats, I really went to work. Normally, I don't need a lot of loosening up before a practice; but that morning I did as much extra jogging as I could. When Coach Rauch came out, we went through the regular fundamentals of the day. Then we broke up into groups to run some plays—and I got my most pleasant surprise of the training season.

Until that morning, the first-team backfield had included Wayne Patrick at fullback and Max Anderson at halfback, with Jack Kemp, Tom Flores, and James Harris rotating at quarterback, depending largely on which of them were injured. But when the coach called out the first team to run some plays, he called Bill Enyart, James Harris, and me—an all-rookie backfield. Privately I had guessed that this might be the backfield of the Bills' future, but I hadn't expected it to take shape that week. All three of us were taken by surprise.

Enyart, a 240-pound running back whom I had played against when he was at Oregon State, had been the Bills' second-round draft choice. Some critics had been dubious about his speed, but there were no questions about his attitude. He was one of the hardest working and most modest guys in camp. Bill looked like a big old farm boy, with a huge smile and short blond hair. He had a funny way of speaking that made him sound like a real hick; sometimes it was hard to believe that he was a Phi Beta Kappa. When the coach called his name, Bill was the most shocked-looking guy on the field.

The naming of James Harris was an even bigger surprise. There was little question about his ability; in his workouts and game appearances, he had shown a great arm and good poise when he was rushed. But several things had seemed to be standing in James's way. First, he still had a lot to learn about the Rauch system, which was much more complex than the one he had directed at Grambling. Second, he still tended to drill some of his passes too hard, causing receivers to drop them when they were on target; he had to develop the touch that comes largely with experience. Third, no pro coach had ever put himself on the spot by opening a season with a black quarterback, much less a black rookie. So Coach Rauch's decision to move James to the first team was both bold and unexpected.

Most people had probably assumed that I would be placed on the first team by that time, but after sitting through those game films, I felt almost as surprised and delighted as Enyart and Harris must have been. The coach's confidence in me gave me even more incentive to practice hard, and I felt that the workout went exceptionally well. It was the best Monday practice I'd been through, and afterwards when the coach asked the quarterbacks and wide receivers to stay out for a while, Enyart and I also stayed around and did a few more laps.

Everything seemed beautiful as Bill and I drove from the stadium back toward the hotel that was the team headquarters downtown. I had watched Sestak and Flint and some of the other veterans go, and now I felt that I was seeing the positive side of their departure—the youth movement with which the coach planned to replace them. A lot could still happen in two weeks, but it seemed possible that Bill, James, and I would open the season, with another rookie, Bubba Thornton, at flanker. We knew that we would make mistakes and have difficulties, as all rookies must, but we also had a lot of exciting progress to look forward to. Even when I learned that two other rookies—Julian Nunamaker and J. C. Collins—had been placed on waivers and wouldn't be a part of our youth program, I wasn't too upset. Both had been more or less assured that if they were claimed, the waivers would be withdrawn and they would still be part of the Bills' future.

Then I stopped in at the hotel to check my messages and met a few of the other guys. One was Henry King, the defensive back who had been a friend of mine for years in San Francisco. Henry had been battling several backs for one of the last spots in the secondary, and I had been rooting hard for him. I knew that Rauch would still be cutting one more defensive back, but from the way practices had been going, I had thought it would be another young guy named Jerome Lawson. In the hotel lobby, John Pitts, our strong safety, came over to talk with me, and Henry started to join us. Then he just sort of waved and walked away. I thought he was waving at me to come with him; but when I started, he just signaled me to go on. Then Ben Gregory came over and told me:

Jerome Lawson had been cut as I'd expected, but Henry had been cut, too.

The reason that both of them had been let go was that Hagood Clarke, a veteran safety, had decided to come out of retirement. That confused me. Clarke was twenty-seven and he had lost his job to Pitts, yet they were bringing him back to be a substitute instead of keeping a younger guy with a future. Coach Rauch had explained it easily to the press: "We're not committed simply to youth or age, but to getting the best team possible." That made sense, but when you're in the middle of a team, watching your friends get shuffled in and out, it isn't always as easy to comprehend such general plans. So I couldn't help feeling shocked and a little mad. Henry was a sensitive, sentimental person, and I knew he'd be taking it hard. I wished that I could find him and say something to make him feel better—but I knew that there really wasn't anything to say. At that moment I understood a little more about how Maguire and Day must have felt when Flint and Sestak left.

The next morning I was exposed to another fact of pro football life, the trade. It wasn't quite as painful, but it was definitely more expensive. Richard Trapp, a second-year man from Florida, had been a starting wide receiver as a rookie; but he had lost his position to Bubba Thornton during training. So most of the guys weren't very shocked when he was traded to the San Diego Chargers; it just happened to catch me unawares. When I walked into the locker room, defensive end Ron McDole said, "Hey O.J., did you collect?"

"What do you mean?"

"Trapp's gone to San Diego," he laughed. "You better catch the next plane." It happened that Trapp, one of the regulars in our card games, owed me $500. Everyone thought it was very funny that he'd left before I could collect. Well, almost everyone—there were a few other guys he owed, too.

Another thing affected me more seriously that morning: some of the players were saying that the coach had picked a new kicker off the waiver lists and was thinking about making some changes. Our placekicker, a quiet guy named Bruce Alford, had been in a slump, so I could understand why Coach Rauch might be shopping around. But what really bothered me was the rumor that he was looking for someone who could punt as well as placekick. That would have meant the end for Maguire. As usual, there was logic behind the coach's reasoning. Alford and Maguire were occupying two spots on the roster, while a kicker who could do both jobs would leave one spot free for some other use. But I still hadn't reached the point where I could accept such logic without emotion. To me, Paul Maguire was invaluable to the Bills. I didn't think that somebody who could kick the ball 80 yards would do as much for the rest of us as Maguire did with his jokes and his spirit. Several of the veterans reassured me that Maguire was untouchable and told me not to worry. But the very thought of losing Maguire added to my confusion about exactly where the Bills were heading.

I had to leave practice early that day because some lawyers and bankers had to settle a few details about my contract. I felt disappointed about it because I was having a very good workout—and also because I had hoped to spend the week getting everything out of my mind but football. Nobody seemed annoyed by my departure, but I was starting to get a little impatient with myself. I appreciated the necessity of my various financial dealings and outside commitments, but there were times when they were a drag to carry out.

Shortly after I left the bank—with a few more dollars safely accounted for—I was struck by another of the countless contrasts between the haves and have-nots of the sport. Driving through town, I stopped at a barber shop that was a hangout for the blacks on the club. As I got out of my Corvette, I noticed a car across the street with California license plates. The back seat was piled high with trunks and clothing; two girls sat in the front, just kind of gazing toward the barber shop. Booker Edgerson, the veteran cornerback who was a fixture in the black section of Buffalo, was inside the shop chatting with the barbers. I asked him who the girls were, and he told me that one of them was Jerome Lawson's wife. Jerome was the defensive back who had been cut the day before.

I had not been especially close to Jerome Lawson, a second-year man who had been on the Bills' taxi squad for most of the 1968 season. But suddenly I felt as if I knew him very well. I looked out the window at his wife and a very unhappy story fell into place. Obviously Jerome had decided, a few days earlier, that he was going to hang on with the Bills. So he had told his wife to pack up and come ahead to join him, and she had probably been on the road someplace when he got the word that he was cut. So here she was, sitting in a car on the main street of a strange city, 3000 miles from her job in L.A., and a million miles from what she had expected to find.

The next day Jerome told me that he was going to get a tryout in the Canadian League. But he had very little money—only the $100 game checks he had collected for his two months of work—and naturally he couldn't take anything for granted. So in order to get her job back, his wife had already started to drive back to L.A. For Roberta Lawson, the glamorous, high-finance world of pro football had turned into a grueling 6000-mile drive and one big disappointment.

It made me think of how lucky I was to be able to give some security to my own wife. I had been worrying about our apartment building, which was so new that it wasn't landscaped and a thick layer of dust blew around where there should have been grass. I was concerned about having things cleaned up when Marguerite arrived and having some friends ready to greet her so she wouldn't feel lonely in a new town. And I was naturally apprehensive about the effects of the cultural shock that hits anyone moving from California to Buffalo. But when I saw Roberta Lawson, those concerns about Marguerite began to seem unimportant. At least she and Arnelle, our little daughter, had a definite future—as well as a community of avid football fans ready to welcome them.

The prospect of my homecoming in Los Angeles must have turned me around a little because I went out and bought one of the flashiest outfits I've ever owned. The jacket was an Edwardian cut, with a red, white, and blue plaid pattern; I wore it with blue bell-bottoms, a dark blue shirt, and a loud tie. It was pretty special to me, since I was known as a fairly straight dresser; in fact, the more I looked at it, the prouder I felt. But when I boarded the plane with it on, the rest of the guys started getting on me.

"At last we get a glimpse of the real O.J.," said Tippy Day. "Boys, he didn't think Buffalo was ready for this Hollywood look."

The others chimed in and said they expected to be guided to all the high spots of Hollywood, and then Tippy added, "I hope O.J. enjoys this Hollywood weekend because he won't look so mod next week when I shave his head." That was a ritual that all the Bills' rookies go through before the opening game. I laughed about it with Tippy, but privately I was hoping to talk to him later about it. I had a commercial to do for Chevrolet and a picture spread to do for another magazine, and I really wanted to do them with the long natural I'd been growing all summer. All I wanted to ask for was a two-week delay in the head-shaving ceremony. Fat chance. Those outside commitments would make it all the more fun for the guys to cut me down to size with their head-shaving ritual.

The five-hour plane ride to L.A. passed quickly, with Tippy and Maguire keeping everybody loose and laughing. When we arrived, I smoothed out my beautiful jacket, straightened my tie, and prepared for my grand return to California. I walked off the plane feeling like a million dollars; despite all the wisecracks, I was sure that everybody was impressed with my new image. A girl from American Airlines was waiting inside the terminal to greet us, and I immediately saw her checking out my threads. Then she rushed up to me and said in a voice everybody on the team could hear, "O.J., what have they done to you? You used to look so *nice* when you lived out here."

I recovered my composure enough to smile at her and say, "You don't like it? I think it's pretty sharp." By now half the team was gathered around.

"Without a doubt," the girl said sweetly, "that is the ugliest coat I've ever seen."

I took the coat off and didn't even wear it on the bus to the hotel. That was the end of my new image; I never put the damn thing back on. But Maguire and the rest of the guys never let me forget about it.

Robert James and I had a big room that adjoined the one shared by Tippy and Marlin Brisco. Robert, who was from some tiny town in the South, was dying to see all the tourist attractions, so he went out on the Sunset Strip to look around. Marlin had some friends to meet, and Tippy, who had spent one season in San Diego, had his usual group of well-wishers waiting to see him. The minute I could, I grabbed a taxi and headed for the USC campus. It was about eight o'clock in the evening when the cab approached the campus on Hoover Street, and I saw a bunch of the football players wandering over toward Founders Hall, where we always had our meetings. I jumped out of the cab, and the guys rushed over to say hello.

I was glad to see everybody—and I was impressed by what I saw. A group of guys that I had known as good friends and good athletes had been transformed over the summer into what I knew would be one of college football's best defenses. By the end of the season they were recognized as *the* best. They called themselves The Wild Bunch and The Five Blacks of Granite, and they smothered everybody, including Michigan in the Rose Bowl. Al Cowlings, my best friend, looked as strong as ever; he didn't seem to have softened up a bit just because he was driving my Corvette around town. The Chevrolet people had given me one car in L.A. and then another in Buffalo, and Al was using my L.A. car while I was gone. Charlie Weaver and Jimmy Gunn also looked as lean and quick as they had been—just the type of linemen that Coach McKay likes.

But the ones who really surprised me were Bubba Scott and Tody Smith. Bubba had weighed about 260 when I had last seen him; we used to call him Piggy and Sherbet Jowls. He never stopped eating, and he would gulp sherbet down by the quart. But he had obviously spent the summer slimming down, and he weighed about 230. Compared to the pros I'd been watching, he actually seemed a little small, but the coaches must have been overjoyed at his condition. Tody Smith, Bubba Smith's little brother, had also shown tremendous enthusiasm by cutting his weight from about 270 to 238. There were some stories in the papers about whether SC could get along without me, but looking at those guys, I knew that they'd have no trouble at all.

Soon they all had to drift off to some team meetings, but I waited around, and finally I saw old Marv Goux. Coach Goux was more or less the symbol of USC to me.

He had recruited me and kept me in line for two years, and every time I didn't act as if everything was going perfectly, he'd remind me, "Don't forget, O.J., you could have chosen Utah State when they recruited you. Then you'd be the biggest man in Logan, Utah, right now." I was very happy to see Coach Goux, but he was a man who controlled his emotions very carefully, and if he was glad to see me, it wasn't very obvious. "Hey stud, how's it going?" he said, as if he'd seen me the day before. Then he invited me into the defensive meeting and I joined Al and Bubba Scott in the meeting room. It was nice to be back, but after a few minutes, I started thinking about some other people I should be looking up in L.A.; in his uncanny way, Coach Goux seemed to read my mind and told me to take off if I felt like it.

Outside, I ran into Jack Ward, the USC trainer and one of my favorite people on campus. When I had arrived at SC, the training room was strictly business. No one was allowed in except injured players who needed treatment. But Earl McCullouch and I were always kidding around in the locker room, and we started hanging out in the trainer's room, too. It set a trend because everybody plays around the training room now. And Jack Ward was not only a great trainer but also a good poker-playing and horse-playing friend. Talking to Jack, I couldn't help comparing USC to Buffalo, where the trainers are good guys, but the training room is all business. It was one more understandable difference between college and pro ball, but seeing old Jack made me miss some of the good times at USC a little more.

Cookie Gilchrist, the great Bills' running back of 1962-1964, had picked up Tippy Day that evening and taken him to a party at Jim Brown's home in Hollywood Hills. When Tippy and I met back at the hotel, we stayed up and talked for a while about Cookie and Jim as well as my

SC friends; Tippy and I were from completely different generations of football, but we were becoming as close as any two athletes could get. Whatever else happened to my pro career, I already considered it worthwhile because I'd gotten to meet a man like Tom Day.

The Ram game was one of those weird, frustrating experiences that became all too familiar as the year progressed. For one half, I thought that everything was finally falling into place for us; in the second half, everything just fell apart. I was a little nervous before the big L.A. crowd, but I lost that nervousness in the simplest way; I threw a very good block on Deacon Jones. For years I had watched and read about the Deacon, probably the best pass rusher in the NFL. In the first period I was pass-blocking and saw him coming at me, and I managed to cut him down. I didn't know it at the time, but that would turn out to be the high point of the game for me. I also returned a kickoff 85 yards for what I thought was a touchdown, and it was great to hear that roar that I'd heard so many times in college in the Coliseum. But the referee ruled that I had stepped out of bounds back near midfield and I had to settle for a 41-yard return.

James Harris had a good first half, showing poise under a hard pass rush and throwing the ball effectively. I think the rest of us responded to James's leadership, and we executed well; we were behind, 17-13, at half time, but we were in the game. Then Jackie Kemp came in and we seemed to collapse, offensively and defensively. We kept giving the Rams opportunities and they kept taking advantage, and the final score was 50-20. It was the most humiliating moment of my life. I had never lost a game by that kind of score, even in high school when we lost fairly often, and I had never lost in the Coliseum. My visions of a triumphant homecoming were rudely shattered. I had carried the ball only seven times for 20 yards —for a total of exactly nineteen carries in four games. West Coast fans, used to seeing me handle the ball nineteen times in a single half, must have wondered what was going on; I was wondering too, but I kept hoping that by the time we returned to the West Coast, I would be doing more and doing it better. I had no idea at the time that after our regular season games in Oakland and San Diego, I'd wish that the Bills had never set foot in California.

That night I flew up to San Francisco to pick up Marquerite and Arnelle, and on Sunday we flew back to our new home in Buffalo. Marquerite managed to pack enough stuff to support an army, but the American Airlines people were so nice about it that I was even ready to forgive that girl who had ridiculed my jacket. At the Buffalo airport, I wanted to rent a station wagon so I could lug all the trunks home, but my driver's license had expired. Luckily there was a man on the same flight who was a friend of Tom Day's—you run into friends of Tippy's almost everywhere around Buffalo—and he used his license to rent the car. When we drove up to our apartment house, I could see Marquerite's face drop. She was uneasy about leaving California anyway, and when she saw the little dirt road and dusty parking lot outside the building, I thought she wanted to turn right around and go back. It was breezy and the dust was swirling; there was a thin layer of dirt on everything as we walked from the car to the lobby; I wished that they had managed to plant just enough grass to hold a little of the dirt on the ground. There were no rugs in the lobby yet, and the elevator was still draped with temporary padding; we rode up in uneasy silence to our fifth floor apartment. When I finally opened the door, I was relieved to see Marquerite smile again. The time I had devoted to getting the furniture set up was well worth it. The apartment was big, bright, and clean, and she breathed a sigh of relief. Maybe the next few months wouldn't be too hard for her after all.

With the season approaching, our practices were switched from the stadium to a high school field called Houghton Park, an undistinguished little place that was, among other things, a spy's paradise. I knew that Coach Rauch, who had worked for the master spy and counter-spy Al Davis, in Oakland, wasn't happy about the fact that bystanders could easily gather around the practice site; but obviously he didn't have much choice. I had never been to the new field, and I knew there was a fine for being late, so I arranged for Tippy to take me that first morning. I started to worry when he was a few minutes late himself, but when he arrived, he was laughing. "I just wanted to scare you a little," he said. "I wanted you to think I might have forgotten about you." I was still worn out from my trip and it was early in the morning; I couldn't think of anybody else other than Tippy who would have been laughing and joking at that hour.

After practice, Tippy helped me carry all Marquerite's trunks from the station wagon into the apartment. Then he stopped to visit with us. Arnelle was only nine months old at the time and she was still pretty shy; in fact, when Ben Gregory came in and picked her up, she cried like mad. But she took to old Tom on the spot. He picked her up and started playing games with her and she couldn't stop laughing. When he finally put her down, she crawled right back to him and made him take her again. Marquerite and I couldn't recall ever having seen Arnelle act so outgoing. She really fell for Tippy.

Tom and Barbara Day came over again that night, along with some friends of theirs from around the city. They talked about how well Buffalo fans treated the players and how much fun you could have in a smaller city like Buffalo. Marquerite and I weren't completely convinced by any means, but our outlook was brightening up quite a bit. When he left, Tom offered to drive me to practice the next morning, but I wanted to try and find it on my own. I told him I'd see him there, if I made it.

Tuesday, September 9, 1969: I could win Super Bowls and Most Valuable Player awards and rushing titles, and no single date will ever burn itself into my mind the way that one did. If training camp was my indoctrination, the first step in my education as a pro football player, then September 9 was the day I passed my first final exam. It was the day I understood, overwhelmingly, that this game could never be the kind of free-spirited fun it was in college; it was the day I realized that this boy's game, played by grown men for big money, could be as cold and cruel as any business in the world.

We had a team meeting in the morning; I was just leaving it when I heard a strange voice calling me. I looked and found Tippy, dressed in street clothes instead of sweats, sitting alone on a bench. He managed to smile, but his voice was so strained I could hardly hear him, and when the words came out, I didn't believe what he was saying; "Come over here, man. This is it for me. The end, pal. I'm done."

I felt as if I'd been punched in the gut. Tom Day. A fixture in Buffalo, a great friend; along with Maguire, the only real life on the team. Cut. Placed on waivers to make room for younger men. But what younger player would fill Tippy Day's place on the Bills? I was speechless. I stared at the floor for a long minute, then looked back at Tippy. He was still smiling. "Don't let it get you, O.J. It's got to come sometime to all of us. You better go, you'll be late for the workout."

I worked out hard, hoping that some good action would

snap me out of my depression. But I could hardly concentrate on what I was doing. I looked around and I couldn't understand how everybody could go on with business as usual. That was the only professional thing for the guys to do, of course, but I wasn't enough of a professional yet. Each time I thought of Tippy sitting on that bench, the five years or so that I planned to stay in football seemed longer and longer. When we got back into the locker room, I felt like shouting at the guys, "Don't you realize what's happened? Tippy Day is gone." But naturally they did realize, and maybe some of them felt as bad as I did. In pro football, you just didn't shout about those things.

It was the day for the traditional head-shaving of the rookies, and with Tippy gone, a defensive tackle named Bob Tatarek shaved me. Tatarek and I hadn't been very friendly all along and I thought he tried to be a little rougher than necessary, but I didn't seem to care enough to get annoyed. I also thought about the commercials and pictures that I would have to do with a bald head, but suddenly they didn't seem very important either. All I knew was that Tippy Day was no longer a Buffalo Bill. And worse yet, not a damn person seemed to care.

Chapter Seven

Opening Day

Four days before the opening game against the Jets, I got my familiar Number 32 back; Gary McDermott, who had been wearing 32, was one of the last preseason cuts. Although I was glad to be wearing 32 again, I was naturally unhappy about the way I got it. Yet somehow those final cuts didn't affect me as much as some of the earlier ones. One of the last guys to go was Charley Ferguson, an end who was a good friend; the other was Gary, who'd been so good about helping me learn the plays. Ordinarily both cuts would have bothered me quite a bit, but what had happened to Tippy had drained me of most of my emotions. I viewed the final cuts fairly coolly, took my 32 back, and kept my mind on the job ahead.

I was getting pretty edgy, and several little things upset me during the week. Barbara Day told Marquerite that one of her daughters had said to Tippy, "Daddy, I wish O.J. Simpson was my daddy." Tom apparently thought that was very funny, but I wondered if it didn't actually bother him a little. I thought that it would have bothered me, and I wished that the little girl hadn't said it. My own little girl caused her share of trouble the same night; she was just getting the knack of crawling, so she crawled around her crib and yelled all night long. I was up for so long that I fell asleep in the team meeting the next morning. We were watching films of the Jets and I nodded off for a minute. The coach saw it and made a brief comment, but he didn't lean on me too hard and I was grateful.

The kids who hung around our practices also started to get on my nerves. It was the first time in my life that I felt bugged by the kids, and I felt a little guilty about my own reactions. Ever since I was little myself, I've been very conscious of how much an autograph or a handshake means to a kid, and I've always tried to cooperate as much as possible with kids when they ask me for anything. But the Buffalo kids were unbelievable. There seemed to be hundreds of them waiting every time I went in or out of practice, yanking at my clothes and milling around in front of me. I tried to sign as many autographs as I could, but I also had places to go; I couldn't just stand there for hours. That week I decided that I finally had to draw the line. I signed as many autographs as time would permit, but when I had to go, I shoved my way through the crowd, got to my car, and slowly but surely inched it through the mob. After years of doing everything the kids asked of me, it wasn't easy to change my habits, but I didn't seem to have much choice. After all, I was a professional now.

During one interview that week, I was asked a question that really got to me: "Don't you feel that you owe a lot to the game of football?" A week earlier, that query might have seemed innocuous enough; but in the light of the events of the last few days, the question upset me. Football was a good game and I had never felt mad at it—but I didn't think that I owed it very much either. "I don't owe football anything," I snapped. "What you get out of football is what you put into it, and when you stop putting anything in, it doesn't give you anything back for nothing. When you can't produce any more, you won't find the game doing you any favors. Ask Henry King or Tom Day."

My answer actually shocked me a little. Perhaps I hadn't even realized how drastically my attitude was changing. But I didn't want to retract what I had said. I had never felt so strongly before, but I knew that I would keep feeling that way as long as I remained in pro ball.

As the pregame tension increased, I was glad that Maguire was still around to keep things loose. It rained very hard before one practice, and Coach Rauch was obviously concerned about missing some work so close to the opening game. We worked out in the rain and things were pretty gloomy until Maguire yelled, "Coach Rauch, haven't you read Clause Six of O.J.'s contract? It says that he doesn't have to practice in the rain."

Practices went well enough for me to honestly believe that we could upset the world champion Jets. The rookie backfield stayed intact, and I got the distinct impression that we were finally going to try to establish a running attack. We spent a lot of time on running plays and they seemed to work well; meanwhile, James Harris seemed to gain more stature each day as a quarterback. James was possibly the first black quarterback in recent years who had what the pros look for. Marlin Briscoe, who had quarterbacked some games for Denver the year before and had joined the Bills as a wide receiver, was too small to see over a lot of the changing defensive linemen. Eldridge Dickey of Oakland had great ability, but he seemed too cocky; he was in such a hurry to take over that he never really adapted himself to the Raiders' system, and I understand that was why he was cut. Harris was different, a very modest and unassuming personality.

If he made it as a leader, it would be as a John Unitas or a Bart Starr type, not as a Joe Namath.

Harris had another important factor going for him: unlike so many potential black quarterbacks over the years, he was not a great all-around athlete. He was a slow runner and had suffered a knee operation; there was no way he could be converted into a wide receiver or defensive back—the fate of many would-be black quarterbacks. He would rise or fall as a quarterback—and most of us were becoming convinced that he would rise. The first time he threw a pass in one of our exhibitions, I heard Maguire say, "Damn, that bastard can throw the football." Nobody could disagree. And Harris's poise under pressure was extraordinary for a rookie. He had shown as much ability to throw under a rush as anyone I'd seen in our exhibition games, with the exception of Unitas himself. The challenge of starting a career against the world champion defense would place even more pressure on him, but I couldn't help feeling that James would handle himself very well.

Coach Rauch had a rule that required the whole team to stay at a hotel on the eve of every game. We had the choice of attending a movie or simply hanging around our rooms until the 11:00 P.M. curfew. Some of the veterans were annoyed by this regulation. "If we don't know by now to go to bed on time the night before a game," said Booker Edgerson, "I don't think it will do much good to start checking up on us now." But nobody complained too seriously because Rauch was obviously instituting a lot of the customs that had helped him at Oakland— and it was hard to argue with the Raiders' success.

I checked into the hotel just before the 6:30 deadline and decided to skip the movie—it was *Midnight Cowboy,* which I'd already seen—and just hang around. I wandered a block down the road to the motel in which the Jets were staying, hoping to find Mike Battle. When he wasn't around, I settled into my room and turned on a Canadian football game on television. A few minutes later I heard a knock and a shout: "Razor!" That was Battle's nickname—because when he turned sideways he was as thin as a blade—and every time we got together, we yelled it at one another. Mike was one of the greatest guys—and one of the toughest—that I'd ever met in football. He had no business making it with the Jets, just as he'd really had no business being a star safety for USC. He weighed about 170 pounds and wasn't fast. But he would fight anybody, on or off the field, and his belligerence was enough to overcome all his shortcomings.

The Jets had picked him as an afterthought in the twelfth round of the draft, making him the 311th college player selected out of our class. Nobody in New York thought that this slow, skinny kid could possibly make it; but at USC, we knew better. Mike showed the Jets very quickly that he was an ideal man for special teams or "suicide squads" because the only way he knew how to play football was suicidal. He loved to hurl himself into the midst of pileups full of men almost twice his size, and on punt returns he didn't know what a fair catch was. He made his name once and for all in New York during the big preseason game between the Jets and the Giants. The Jets killed the Giants, 37-14, in a game so onesided that it wasn't even memorable; but the one play no one could forget was Mike's touchdown punt return, which included a high hurdle over the final would-be tackler. I knew that he had also hurdled at least one table in a bar that was a Jets' hangout, as well as doing his famous glass-eating routine for his new teammates. The veteran Jets had been so impressed by his stunts that they named him Joe Don, after Joe Don Looney, who was generally considered the craziest football player around until Battle arrived.

Mike had been looking for me partly because he was anxious to pay back some money I had loaned him. On the night before he was to leave California for the Jets' camp, he had been arrested. He had a lot of old traffic tickets he hadn't paid, and the detectives found him at a going-away party in Long Beach. He had thought about making a break for it through a back window, but his father had talked him out of it. "How would it look," his dad had told him, "if you made the Jets and came back here for the third game of the season in San Diego—and two cops ran out and grabbed you under the goal posts as you were waiting for the opening kickoff?" So Mike had given himself up, and bail had been set at $500. He called me and I went down and paid it because I didn't want him to hurt his chances by reporting late to camp; it would have been difficult to explain the delay to Weeb Ewbank.

Mike promised that he would send me the money that week, but I told him to take his time. I was in no hurry for it, and I wanted him to get himself settled first and then send it when he had it to spare. But Mike is a very proud guy and he hates to owe anybody anything, so I knew I'd be seeing the cash fairly soon.

As we exchanged stories about the training season, Mike mentioned that some of the Jet veterans had been getting on him about me, saying that I would be the biggest bust in history. He said that linebacker Larry Grantham, in particular, had predicted, "O.J. will fall flat on his face in pro ball." I hoped that I would get Grantham one-on-one on a pass play sometime during the game.

The Jets as a group sounded pretty cocky before the game. A lot of it stems from Namath's style, and it's a healthy attitude for them to have. The fact that they

weren't the least bit awed by the Baltimore Colts or the
NFL mystique certainly had a lot to do with their Super
Bowl victory—and they were carrying that confident approach into the next season. Still, a few remarks were
hard to take. Ben Gregory knew some people who had
been in the bar of the Jets' motel that night, and tight
end Pete Lammons had stopped in. He had been telling
everyone in the place, "I hope nothing happens to that
John Pitts. I've been watching him on films, and I'm dying
to get at him. Please keep him healthy for me." We were
all hoping that Pitts, the strong safety, would be healthy
enough to get some good shots in at Lammons.

The game was in many ways a preview of what we
would go through all season. We did some very good
things and had moments when we seemed on the verge
of a tremendous victory. But we made some dreadful
mistakes that no team can afford if it expects to win. Our
defense was much stronger than our offense; our running
game didn't really get established, and our passing was
erratic. As things turned out, these statements would
echo around us throughout the long season; but at the
time, it seemed as if we had a right to be encouraged. We
were tied with the world champions with only ten minutes
remaining, and we lost not only because of our own errors,
but because Joe Namath was Joe Namath—a quarterback who comes up with some incredibly big plays. It
didn't strike me as anything to be ashamed of.

The pregame locker room atmosphere surprised me. I
had anticipated a quiet, tense, charged-up scene, but it
was as relaxed as it had been before our exhibition games.
Again I had to remind myself that professionals don't need
rituals or pep talks; they get ready in their own ways.
Most of the guys chatted about everything but the game,
trying to keep themselves loose. And Maguire entertained

everybody with a string of speeches and remarks. Most of his comments were directed at J.C. Collins, the popular linebacker who had been waived but was still with the club. J.C., who is black, had been married the day before to a white girl. "I hear that her parents are furious about the match," Maguire announced. "They're Catholic, and they never dreamed that their daughter would marry a Protestant."

The Buffalo fans, who are among the most knowledgeable in football, forgot local feelings and gave the Jets a standing ovation when they were introduced. Like the veteran players, the AFL fans had taken a lot of abuse over the years; they really poured out their gratitude to the team that had finally knocked off the NFL in the Super Bowl. On their first drive the Jets looked like the champs, too, moving inside our ten-yard-line. But two big tackles by Lammons's "pigeon," Pitts, helped to stop them at the two, and they settled for a field goal. I trotted out to receive my first kickoff in a regular season pro game.

Waiting for the kick, I was thinking, "I hope it comes to me." Under our kickoffs, Bubba Thornton always called, "You, you," or "Me, me," and this time I was desperately hoping he would be yelling for me to take it. We had done very well on our returns in preseason games, and I had visions of taking that first one all the way. The kick floated down the middle; Bubba hesitated for a second and then called, "You, you." I took it in stride on the six; 25 yards later a tackle named Roger Finnie rudely ended my dream of a quick touchdown. In a way, it felt good to get hit hard. My adrenaline was pumping; all the thoughts of the past six weeks were pushed out of my mind. At last, the season was on.

I gained 2 yards on the first play. Then we lost the ball on a fumble by Enyart and got it back on a great interception by Butch Byrd, who's always a nemesis to Namath. On the next play, I got a kind of baptism. On a sweep around left end I broke away for 22 yards. Jim Hudson, their big safety knocked me out of bounds. He hit me good and hard, which was fine, but then as we rolled over he kicked out at me. I didn't know whether he was disgusted by my gain or just trying to get me, but I jumped up and flipped the ball at him and we exchanged a few words. When I thought about it, I was sorry I'd said anything; I didn't want to get a quick reputation as a guy who couldn't take a little punishment. So when I had a chance, I said, "Sorry about that." Hudson said, "Nothing to it, man. Good run." But by that time he could afford to be cheerful. The Jets had taken charge.

On that same drive I ran a good long pass pattern. Harris's pass was short, but the linebacker, John Neidert, shielded my eyes and then bumped me, so we drew a long interference penalty that set up our first field goal. From then on, unfortunately, we leaned on our defense. We messed up a number of plays with mixups in the backfield, largely because James hadn't learned to bark his signals loud enough. He tended to lapse into the kind of quiet drawl he uses in normal conversation, and it was impossible to hear him above the crowd noises. In addition, his passes were tantalizingly close but inches off target. He proved beyond doubt that he had a pro arm, but he still lacked the delicate touch that could have turned some near-misses into touchdowns.

I had been curious about how their linebackers would play me—particularly Grantham, who was so sure that I'd be a flop. The majority of linebackers will try to clothesline you, coming at your head with their forearms to try to knock you down or intimidate you before you can run a pattern. But the Jets, who have some of the fastest linebackers in football, may fancy themselves as being a little faster than they actually are; they don't bump as much, and they'll try to run with you. The first time Grantham tried that, I told James in the huddle, "He's trying to stay with me alone. Just put it up for grabs and I'll beat him." I did beat him once that way, but the ball was thrown to the other side. On the way back I said to Grantham, "I had you that time."

"I let up," he said, "because I thought we'd gotten your quarterback."

"That could've been a costly misjudgment."

"Could've been, but it wasn't."

I never did get a chance to burn Grantham, but I earned a little respect from him. The first time he hit me, I looked straight at him, and I think he expected me to curse at him or something. "Way to come across, man," I said. "Good hit." He looked a little shocked.

The Jets had scratched out a 9-3 lead when Broadway Joe staged one of his most dramatic shows. Midway in the second period, Bob Tatarek got to Namath just as he threw an incomplete pass; Tatarek and Winston Hill, the Jets' 285-pound offensive tackle, collided and fell into Joe's leg. On the bench we were all cheering the good pass rush—until we saw that Namath, getting up very slowly, was hobbling badly on an injured right knee. Nobody in pro ball wants to see a star like Joe, who's done so much for the entire sport, put out of action. Tatarek, who undoubtedly wasn't thinking about what he was doing, stood over Namath for a moment, clapping his hands in triumph; Harry Jacobs quickly pulled him away. The exuberant gesture hadn't looked very sporting, and I'm sure Tatarek would have regretted it if Namath had been seriously hurt. But after a timeout, Joe returned to the huddle.

Everyone familiar with the Namath style knew just what to expect: Getting up off the deck, Joe would go for the bomb. No one was more prepared for it than Booker

Edgerson, and he covered Don Maynard like a blanket as Maynard headed for the end zone. But when Joe threw, he got a tremendous break. The ball was short, Maynard had to slow down for it—and as Booker tried to slow down with him, Booker tripped. It threw him off stride just long enough for Maynard to grab the ball and score. It was a freak play that never should have worked. But that was Joe Namath. Somehow he made things work for him.

The score was 19-3 late in the third quarter when our defense got us back into the game. John Pitts picked up a fumble and ran it to the Jets eight-yard-line, and Jack Kemp came off the bench to throw a touchdown pass. Then George Saimes, our great free safety, intercepted a pass and returned it 28 yards to the Jets' sixteen. I scored the touchdown on an 8-yard trap play to make it 19 to 16. Two plays later linebacker Paul Guidry intercepted another pass and took it 39 yards to the Jets' four. A touchdown at that point would have put us ahead; but we settled for a field goal and a tie score, because of one of those crazy mistakes that would kill us all year.

In the huddle, with that cavernous old stadium shaking with noise, Kemp called a "19-crack," a sweep on which the outside receivers crack back on the linebackers, allowing me to go wide. Maybe it was because he hadn't been getting much playing time, but Jack had called a play that just won't work against a nine-man-line goal-line defense. He realized it at the line of scrimmage and changed to another sweep, but there still weren't enough blockers on the left side to make it work. I found myself staring right at the cornerback and safety when I got the ball; I tried to hop around and fake them, but I couldn't avoid a 2-yard loss. That threw us back to the six, and two more plays couldn't get us in. So we settled for the tying field goal, and then Namath went to work again.

It was a grim, painful lesson in leadership and composure. Many quarterbacks, flustered by the three quick scores and the interceptions, might have panicked and tried to throw long passes to score quickly. But Joe didn't throw a pass. He called five straight running plays, and Matt Snell ripped through for a touchdown. A few minutes later, linebacker Paul Crane intercepted a soft sideline pass from Kemp and scored easily, and our dramatic charge had evaporated into a 33-19 defeat.

I was quite satisfied with my own play. I missed one blocking assignment badly and caused Harris to get dumped; I also got careless with the ball once and fumbled, setting up a Jet field goal. Watching the films later, I also noticed a few less obvious errors. But I had made a couple of good runs and broken away for 55 yards with one screen pass, so I felt that I was beginning to get into high gear. I was still a little disappointed that I had only carried the ball ten times from scrimmage; I had hoped that we would be a running team, and yet the Jets had run twice as many running plays as we had. But our quarterbacks, especially Harris, were still finding themselves, and I assumed that we'd develop a more balanced attack as we went along. After all, the Bills had used their first two draft picks to get me and Enyart; I was sure they didn't select us just to pass-block.

James Harris was pretty disappointed with his debut. He had completed only three of twelve passes and had been confused by the shifting New York defenses when he tried to call audibles. He had also aggravated a groin injury, and he wasn't sure when he'd be able to play again. I was pleased when Namath took the trouble to talk to James as we left the field. "Don't get down," Joe told him. "This is the hardest defense to read that you'll face all year."

"It *was* hard to read," said James.

"You bet," said Joe. "So be sure it doesn't get you down."

I hoped that James would take Namath's advice, because even his incomplete passes had been thrown so impressively that I was sure he would develop into a good quarterback. I didn't want to see his confidence shaken at that point. In fact, despite the final score, I felt that we had reason to be optimistic. As Coach Rauch pointed out, it had been a case of an experienced team taking advantage of a young team's mistakes. And as we cut down on those mistakes, our young team had a chance to become a damn good one.

Chapter Eight

"Some Things Need To Be Said"

Once the season was under way, I began to feel more at home with the Bills. Just going through the experience of a regular-season game had inevitably drawn us all closer together; I had played enough of a role to consider myself an integral part of the team. We had worked together under fire for one afternoon. We had done a few things well, we had learned how much work lay ahead for us—and the distinction between veterans and rookies was already blurring in my mind. In training camp I had wondered if we all weren't rookies in a sense; I had had difficulty seeing differences between older and younger players. Now I was wondering how many of those differences actually existed. I had watched veterans make mistakes against the Jets just as the rookies did—although perhaps not as many. I had noticed that many veterans seemed to get more upset before the game than the rookies did. It seemed to me that executing, thinking, and preparing for a game were all personal matters. Each individual approached them in his own way, and his age or experience didn't really have too much to do with it. Every game presented a brand new challenge and a brand new situation, and every player going into a game was, in a sense, a rookie on that afternoon.

In small ways, I was learning the rules of conduct in pro football. Running some patterns in practice before our game against Houston, I recalled something I'd done on my second day in camp. We were in a passing drill, with the running backs and ends going out on patterns and the linebackers and defensive backs working on coverage. Once I broke into the open very deep and I was so proud of myself that I yelled to the quarterback to throw me the ball. The minute I'd said it, I realized that this was just a routine drill and I hadn't performed any great feat by getting into the clear. As I walked back, all the guys looked at me and clapped and yelled, "Thataway to yell, O.J." That was Lesson One. They haven't heard me yelling since.

Then a few days before the Houston game, I was joking around with Maguire and some of the other guys when Butch Byrd walked into the locker room wearing a windbreaker that had the lettering "All-Pro" on it. At USC, if anyone ever walked around with "All-Conference" or "All-American" on his clothes or any kind of medal around his neck, he'd never hear the end of it. So I laughed and said, "Hey fellas, look at this. All-Pro. Look at old Butch."

Butch looked at me as if I were nuts, and the whole room became very quiet. "He earned it," said Billy Shaw. "When you earn one, you'll wear it, too."

The guys tried to laugh it off, but I was really embarrassed. Billy was the man I respected most on the Bills, and it stung to hear him put me down. It was another lesson I wouldn't forget. On a team struggling to make itself into a winner, you don't make jokes about men who have made themselves into All-Pros.

On my day off after the Jet game, I went to New York

to participate in a panel for *Sport* magazine on the athletes of the 1970s. I joined Bobby Orr of the Boston Bruins, Westley Unseld of the Baltimore Bullets, and Denny McLain of the Detroit Tigers in a round-table discussion of our respective sports and the directions in which they were going.

McLain, at twenty-five, was the oldest member of the group. He told me about his off-the-field investments and how well they were doing. In retrospect, the conversation was highly ironic. Not only did the companies he was bragging about drag him deep into debt, but he wound up suspended from baseball for half a season for his adventures with gamblers. I was as shocked as any sports fan when that news broke. It seemed unbelievable that a young athlete with so much going for him would be stupid enough to risk it all by getting involved in gambling. For that matter, he was lucky to get off as lightly as he did. But as I read about the way he had messed up his life, I recalled one thing he had said to me. He had said that I was foolish to give up 10 percent of my income to an agent; he handled everything himself, calling in lawyers only when he needed them to draw up specific contracts. I thought, "This guy must be a genius to handle so much." It was typical of Denny's attitude toward everything. He thought he could do everything better than anyone else. It can be a good attitude to have on a playing field, but in other businesses, it can be fatal. Once again I was convinced that at 10 percent of my income, Chuck Barnes was the best investment I had ever made.

I was especially impressed with Bobby Orr, who was only twenty-one but had already been in hockey for a number of years. With the aid of a bright Toronto lawyer named Alan Eagleson, he had negotiated the biggest contract in hockey history when he was just twenty. He and I shared similar views about the need to combine love of a game with financial security. I was very happy later in the year when Bobby had the greatest season that a hockey player ever enjoyed. If there were still a lot of critics who doubted *my* worth, at least Bobby had proven that an athlete can be worth every last dollar he gets paid.

During the panel discussion, I brought up one topic that probably irked Ralph Wilson. Thinking of Jerome Lawson, Henry King, and some of my other friends who had been cut after receiving only a few $100 game checks, I said that if the preseason was going to extend for six games, the players should share more equally in the profits from the games. It was hardly a new complaint; many players have been arguing in favor of higher preseason pay for some time. But after I had spoken out, I realized that I was already losing some of the inhibitions that go with being a rookie.

Watching the game films of the Houston Oilers, we got an interesting glimpse of one side of Coach Rauch. Houston had lost a close game to Oakland the week before, and those were the films we had to study. Naturally most of our attention was focused on Houston, but when the Raiders did something unusual on the films, we could see Rauch's face light up. Normally the coach tried to be as cool as possible about everything. He might get mad on the sideline during the games, but he always tried hard to keep his composure. He usually talked slow and low, trying to make his points in a very calm, direct manner. But as he spoke of the Raiders, his voice changed a little. Once Fred Biletnikoff, the great Oakland receiver, caught a long pass. "They say he doesn't have any speed, they say he's too small," said the coach, "but he always gets the job done for you." His voice trailed off; we weren't even sure he had meant to talk out loud. Moments later Pete Banaszak made a good run, and Rauch spoke out again, "He's not that fast, he's not that great a running back, but he'll come out and knock the crap out of somebody." Whether it was intended or not, the message was clear. Coach Rauch was used to being around winners. He had sacrificed a lot when he left Oakland, and he was anxious to build up something just as good in Buffalo.

As for the Oilers on the films, I was a little surprised at George Webster, the All-Pro linebacker from Michigan State. I hadn't seen George play too much, and from what I had read about him, I had expected to see a guy who was just impossible to stop. But watching the films, I saw that he could be blocked if you went at him low enough. He was certainly a superb player, as everyone had claimed; but he was vulnerable to certain plays. I looked forward to trying to block him and run some pass patterns against him.

We spent most of the week working on the I-formation —a fact that really boosted my spirits. It wasn't exactly the same "I" that we had used at USC; some of the blocking angles and assignments were a little different. But it was basically the same offense that had helped me run for all that yardage in college—an offense that was designed mainly for running the ball. A lot of the guys, especially the offensive linemen, told me that they were looking forward to running the ball more, and nobody was looking forward to it more than I was. Whatever others might have thought, it wasn't just a personal thing. I honestly didn't care if the ball went to me or Bill Enyart or Wayne Patrick, as long as we were determined to establish a ground game. As an individual, I was confident that if I got the ball twenty times or so—instead of the ten times I got it against the Jets—I would gain over 100 yards and possibly break for a few long runs. And considering us as a team, I felt just as strongly that we would improve with more running. After all, I'd played in five games full of passing, and I hadn't played in a winning game yet.

Like almost everyone else in Buffalo, I was sure that our defense would stop the Oilers if we just did our jobs on offense and controlled the ball. I was a little concerned because Pete Beathard, the Oiler quarterback from USC, was a scrambling type, and our defensive linemen were big and strong but not unusually quick. If Houston had any weapon that could hurt us, I was afraid it would be Pete's scrambling; but when you're around the proud Bill defenders, it's hard to get too worried about anyone doing them much harm.

USC opened its season on the day before the Houston game, giving me something to think about during the tense hours before our game. The Trojans were playing Nebraska, and I bet one dinner with Ron McDole, our All-Pro defensive end who went to Nebraska. Ben played at Nebraska, too, but he wouldn't bet because he thought USC would whip them. I managed to get another friendly dinner bet from Marlin Briscoe, who quarterbacked the University of Omaha, and I had a lot of fun telling all the Bills how great the Trojans would be. Then, sitting in our trainers' room, I suddenly decided to call Al Cowlings. I picked up the phone and dialed the L.A. area code, 213, never expecting to get through without being interrupted by a Buffalo operator who would bill me for it. But the call went right through to Al; when Ralph Wilson got the bill, he probably owed the phone company more than McDole's dinner would cost him. Al told me that things weren't going too well; a lot of the offensive guards and backs were hurt. With all the mouthing off that I'd been doing, I would've been pretty embarrassed if USC had been beaten. I told Al that I was really counting on the Wild Bunch.

I needn't have worried. The Trojans opened up a big

early lead and won, 31-21, to start what turned out to be an undefeated season. I hoped that it would also start a great year for my man Cowlings because I was praying that the Bills would draft him so he could join me in Buffalo. I was boosting him at every opportunity to Harvey Johnson, the Bills' director of player personnel. That might have seemed pretty brash for a rookie, but Harve was a hell of a good guy and seemed to like to talk to all the players. He had watched SC during scrimmages and he agreed that Al was a top prospect, but he said that Mike McCoy of Notre Dame rated ahead of him. "At Notre Dame it's easier for a big tackle to look good," I argued. "They play that four-four defense in which all the front four have to do is put on an all-out charge. At USC, our defense is geared primarily to contain and let the linebackers make a lot of tackles. So our linemen have to be quicker and more versatile. If you ask Al to just blow in there straight ahead, he'll be better than McCoy or anyone else because he's so quick."

Looking back on it, that was a pretty pretentious speech. Of course Harve knew more about the Notre Dame and USC styles than I did; that was his business. But he listened cheerfully to my pleas for Cowlings and gave me the impression that he was really interested in what I had to say. I don't think he ever looked on me as a wise rookie, and I enjoyed a lot of lively conversations with him throughout the season. It was easy to understand why Harve, who had stepped in to coach the Bills for the last twelve games of the disastrous 1968 season, was so popular with the players.

Along with a lot of the other players, I was finding it hard to adjust to Coach Rauch's plans for the night before each game. He wanted us together at the movies or in the hotel, which was a fine idea, except that I'd seen all the movies that happened to be playing in town—and just sitting around hotels drove me crazy. So after I checked in at 6:30, I wandered home to lie around and try to relax. At about nine, Barbara Day came over to see Marquerite, and I got dressed to go back to the hotel. On the way out of the apartment, I ran into Ben Gregory, who didn't have to check in because he was on the injured list. "I'm on my way over to that party we heard about," Ben said. "Why don't you drop by with me for a minute."

"That's right over by where Coach Rauch lives," I said. "I guess I have time to stop." I followed Ben to a condominium and we got out of our cars just in time to see two people walking toward us. We thought one of them might be Coach Rauch, so we dashed around the side of the building like little kids. When we saw that the guy wasn't Rauch, we went on into the party. It was a pretty good gathering, including a few other players, and Ben stayed pretty late and had a hell of a time. I just said hello to some people, and then, at 10:30, I headed back to the hotel.

I arrived at three minutes after eleven. My watch had been a little slow and I was three minutes late for curfew. When I walked into the lobby, I saw Ray Jacobs, a big tackle on our taxi squad, who had also been at the party. Then I saw Coach Rauch. For a minute I thought about hiding someplace, but then I realized that it would be pretty stupid because the coach would wait around and find out anyway. So I walked to the elevator, where he was sitting. "Well O.J.," he said, "it's only three after. It's not too late."

I breathed a sigh of relief, assuming that I wasn't going to get fined. As I went up to my room, I was grateful that I was carrying my bag, to at least make it look as if I'd come straight from my home. In the rooms, Enyart and Julian Nunamaker had ordered some sandwiches, so I sat around with them for a few minutes and forgot all about the incident.

The next morning, however, the coach called me over before our pregame meal. "I heard you were at a party over there where I live," he said.

"No," I blurted out, but I quickly decided that it would be very stupid to lie about it. "Well, yeah, I did drop in for a few minutes."

"That place has been under surveillance," he said. "There were known gamblers in there."

That shocked me. Nobody at the party had even mentioned the coming game to me, and I hadn't been drinking or doing anything I was ashamed of. But I was sorry about not being at the hotel where I should have been in the first place, and the coach's statement made me feel worse. I didn't believe that you could be blamed for being at a party where some total stranger turned out to be a gambler, but the fact that I shouldn't have been there anyway didn't leave me much room for argument. I just kept quiet and started putting the whole thing out of my mind.

Concentrating on the game, I was disturbed by one trend I had noticed in our practices. Jack Kemp was one of the best quarterbacks in AFL history and I had a lot of respect for him, but I had begun to notice that often when he dropped back to pass, he already had his mind made up about whom he would throw to. In practice we had run a lot of 28- or 29-play passes, plays on which a back would fake a run or a block and keep going into the secondary. All week I had been wide-open on those plays only to watch him throw to other receivers, even when they were covered. I was hoping that when we ran one of those plays in the game, he would look my way and throw to me because I had a feeling that we could break one of them for a touchdown.

We did run a 29-play pass at one point in the game. But their linebackers were in a stunt and one of them caught me before I could get past the line of scrimmage. I didn't have to worry about Jack failing to see me because I didn't even get out on a damn pattern. He threw in another direction, and it was intercepted. And that summed up the disappointment of the entire game. It seemed slightly incredible, but we didn't even manage to score a touchdown as the Oilers won, 17-3.

As we dressed before the game, I felt increasingly confident. The locker room was a little tense and I thought that we were really gearing ourselves for a big effort. Then Coach Rauch asked for everyone's attention; generally he does this when it is time for a silent prayer, but this time he said, "There are some guys here who want to talk to you." Then he went into the coaches' room and left us alone.

Billy Shaw was the first to speak. Basically, Billy was a man who tried to lead by his actions rather than words, so when he stood up, it impressed everyone. "As you know," he began, "I don't feel that I'm a rah-rah type. But some things need to be said. We have to get out there today and prove to ourselves that we are a football team, that we can win a lot of games. It's not going to be a matter of one or two guys doing a job, it's going to take a whole group working together. But we can win, if we're willing to work hard enough and want it badly enough."

Then, strangely, Paul Maguire joined in. I had assumed that Maguire would never say anything serious in a locker room, but he was dead serious this time. "If we believe that we're a 7-7 club," he said, "we'll be lucky to do even that well. But if we believe that we're a lot better than an ordinary team, we can win a lot of games. It's time we got on the ball and did something."

Harry Jacobs, the defensive captain, added another speech, echoing what Billy and Paul had said, and everybody in the room seemed to be hanging on each word. Then Maguire returned to his old form and interrupted,

"Anyway, as every Buffalo Bill knows, it's a lot more fun drinking when you win than when you lose." There was a pause, as if the guys weren't sure whether to laugh or remain serious. Then Maguire added, "After all, fellas, it's later today than it's ever been." That broke everybody up, and we went out onto the field loose and ready.

The game started beautifully. For the first time since I'd been a Bill, we won the coin toss and received, and during the opening series it seemed that our luck had really changed. Running from the "I," we just manhandled the Oilers. We ran the ball down their throats, Jack threw several timely passes, and we moved to a first down on their six-yard-line. But we couldn't shove the ball over and settled for a field goal and a 3-0 lead.

Houston scored early in the second period with the help of a long punt return by Jerry Levias. We only trailed 7-3, and we were playing well enough to come back and win; but suddenly our pattern changed drastically. After one more series of running plays failed, we started playing volleyball. One drive sputtered with three straight incomplete passes, another fairly strong drive ended with an interception, and still another was killed when tight end Billy Masters caught a pass deep in Oiler territory and then fumbled it away. The officials were very slow with the whistle on that play and it probably shouldn't have been ruled a fumble—but it was, and at half time we found ourselves 4 points behind a team that we had outplayed.

As we left the field at the half, Billy Shaw said to me, "Man, we were running the ball well, doing a job on them. Now we're throwing too much. Let's say something to Jack." As a rookie, I didn't feel that I could say anything to Jack, but I was desperately hoping that Billy would. And I said out loud to all the guys, "Let's run the ball and control the ball, and we can beat these guys."

"We're only behind 7-3," added Billy. "We can come back."

I got pretty worked up, convincing myself that we would go right out and score to take charge of the game. When it was time to start the half, I turned and shouted, "Let's go get 'em, Billy." Then I was hit by a very sick feeling. I saw that Billy Shaw was on the verge of tears.

"It's my leg," he said. "I'm through. Through for the day."

Losing Billy seemed to have an effect on all of us. After the second-half kickoff, Houston controlled the ball for almost eight minutes and finally kicked a field goal. That gave them a 7-point lead and only heightened Jack's determination to pass. And without Billy, our offensive line had trouble protecting him; on one series he was thrown back from our twenty to our goal line. Early in the fourth period, Beathard threw a long touchdown pass to make it 17-3, and we were finished. Facing a brutal pass rush, we attempted one pass after another with no success while time ran out on us.

It was the first time that I felt genuinely mad during a game. It wasn't that Jack wasn't throwing well; he was fairly accurate, but it seemed that every time we got a drive moving, he would pass once too often and something would break down. In the second half I became even more frustrated; we went into a double flanker formation, I drew one-on-one coverage on my patterns—and I never got my hands on the ball. At least four times I was wide-open, but Jack, harassed by that tremendous pass rush, never got a chance to look my way. Once I came to the sideline and Tom Flores said, "You were open, weren't you?"

"I know I was open."

"I told Jack about it. Now you tell him."

I did tell Jack, but he never had a chance to do anything about it. Shortly after we lost Shaw, tackle Paul Costa aggravated a back injury; that left two rookies, Angelo Loukas and Mike Richey, in our offensive line, and the Oilers, blitzing more and more, gave them a very rough afternoon.

I was furious in the locker room after the game. I was annoyed at myself because after expecting to make 100 yards, I had managed only 58 on nineteen carries. I was mad about the way our game plan had fallen apart—and mainly, I was mad because this was a game we should have won. We had had a shot at beating the Jets, but that developed because of several big plays by our defense; overall, we hadn't done enough things well enough to claim that we deserved to win. Against the Oilers, on the other hand, we had shown that we could win. And then we had gone and thrown away three scoring chances near the end of the first half—virtually giving away the ball game.

Generally I like to sit and relax for a few minutes after a game. Then I find myself surrounded by reporters and I answer all the questions, and by the time I get going, an hour will have passed. But after that game I dressed as quickly as I could. I answered the reporters as briefly as possible and left the locker room earlier than I'd ever left one before. Even the kids waiting for autographs seemed to sense my impatience; they asked for a few, but they didn't bug me the way they usually did. When I spotted Marquerite in the crowd, I took her hand and led her to the car without slowing down at all. We drove to the Fairfax Hotel, where Coach Rauch had instituted a custom he had used in Oakland—postgame team parties, win or lose.

I had skipped the party the week before and I felt like skipping it again, but I didn't want any of the guys to think I was a snob or anything. So we went—and I was glad we did. It was a lively scene, and I had a few beers and began to get into a better mood. Marquerite met some of the players' wives for the first time, and everyone seemed friendly and jovial. I wondered how this affair might turn out when we finally won a game; if everyone felt this good after a loss, they'd probably be hanging from the rafters after a victory.

That night I began to feel like a negligent husband. Marquerite was hungry and a little bored, and she wanted to go out for a good dinner and some fun. But I was tired and I had to make a 9:30 P.M. flight to Detroit so I'd be ready to do a Chevrolet commercial early in the morning. So we just went home for a while, and she got pretty mad. I couldn't really blame her. She had been alone all weekend and she would be alone all day Monday, in a town that she was just getting to know. Thinking about that, I felt like pretty much of a heel.

A game like our Houston defeat shatters a lot of illusions, but it also sharpens your vision for what's going on around you. Meditating on the game, I tried hard to figure out just how bad—or how good—we were. Larry Felser, the astute pro football writer for the *Buffalo Evening News*, wrote a piece about a possible "loser's complex" on the Bills, and I wondered if he might have a point. The Bills had lost ten straight regular season games and twenty of their last twenty-two. Felser admitted that any such intangible attitude wasn't as important as "quarterback problems and lack of experience"—but he did make an interesting case. The Bills had an uncanny knack for making big mistakes at crucial moments. Was it the result of some psychological hangup?

I thought about our offensive line. We had an old line, a group of veterans who'd been together through both good and bad years. But they weren't too old: Paul Costa was twenty-seven, Joe O'Donnell, twenty-eight, and Billy Shaw, thirty, and they were all among the better linemen in the league. In fact, age should have been an asset. They should have had the experience to pick out their targets and drive them back. A blocker's first responsibility is to make sure he's got the right guy to block; but even in a new system, veterans should pick that up. Then it's a matter of staying with the block, and that's where we fell short.

Coach Rauch accused me of cutting back too often. But many times on sweeps, I saw nothing but Oilers in front of me. If I'd kept the plays wide, I was just destined to run into their cornerbacks and lose yardage, so I cut upfield to get what I could. I would have loved to stay wide and try to break plays for big yardage, but when I saw defenders sliding off our blockers, I would just cut up and try for first downs.

It seemed to me that our linemen typified the Bills' situation. They were competent, hardworking professionals. But they were doing their jobs without that extra spark that might be the difference between winning and losing. My mind rushed back to the first problem that had hit me in training camp: this team desperately needed a leader. Harry Jacobs kept the defense fired up, but we had no one to get the offense going. I wished that it could be Billy Shaw, but Billy was hurt now, and even when he was playing, he was just a little too quiet and workman-like to provide the lift we needed.

Jack Kemp indicated in the Houston game that he wasn't likely to be the answer. When you have veterans on the line and a rookie in the backfield all saying that we should run and the quarterback still keeps throwing passes, it doesn't exactly qualify him as a strong leader. Jack was a hell of a nice guy and a pleasure to talk to— but I was beginning to wonder whether he really heard what you said to him. Telling him that I had been open on pass patterns had been like talking to a door. Even Dan Durragh, the rookie quarterback who had been in street clothes on the sidelines, had commented on how Jack often had his mind made up before he went back to pass. I didn't think that Kemp could be the leader we sought because too many of us weren't even sure that he should have been playing.

That left it to a younger guy. If James Harris produced, he could have been the man. Or if I came through, it could have been me. At USC, I had been the captain, but I hadn't really done much talking before the games—the coaches had taken care of most of that. Yet before the Houston game I had heard several guys saying, "Come on, O.J., let's break one," and for the first time I realized that they were depending on me. I wondered if it was up to me, a rookie, to try to take charge. The answer didn't come easily; I decided that before I started thinking about talking or leading, I'd better do some more impressive running. But several things did become clear in my mind: We needed someone to get us going, we needed a victory —and we were an angry football team that would soon take that anger out on somebody.

Chapter Nine

A New Ball Game

Maybe it was because I had waited so long for it—through a season-ending tie with Notre Dame in 1968, a loss in the Rose Bowl to Ohio State in my final USC game, a defeat in the Hula Bowl All-Star game; then four exhibition failures and two regular season losses with the Bills. Maybe after a career of winning and succeeding, that streak of defeats put victory in a glorious new perspective for me. Or perhaps it was just the joyous surprise element: The Denver Broncos had been the first team we played that I had really thought might be too strong for us. I guess there were a million thoughts swimming in my head as we finally won a football game, and I'm sure each man on the team felt a million little satisfactions of his own. In any case, our 41-28 win over the Broncos turned a year of frustration into a day of hope. That hope would be short-lived, as things worked out, but its brief intensity left its impression. I had never imagined that winning one game could mean quite so much.

Right after our loss to Houston, I flew to Detroit to do a commercial for Chevrolet. A few months earlier, those commercials and appearances had promised to be interesting as well as lucrative. But after two bitter losses, the plane trip seemed tiring and the commercial was just a long grueling session under hot lights. Once I had looked forward to hustling around on Mondays, fulfilling obligations and advancing my outside interests. Now, feeling like a loser, I longed to transform Monday into a simple day off.

In Detroit I called Earl McCullouch, whose Lions had also suffered a painful defeat that weekend. Talking to my friends on the Lions before the season, I had gotten the distinct impression that they might be taking their opening game with the weak Pittsburgh Steelers too lightly. Unfortunately, I had been correct. They had been upset, in a game that turned out to be the poor Steelers' only win of the season; and my man Earl had dropped a couple of passes in the open.

Earl was living in Detroit with his wife Peggy, which was a story in itself to most of us from L.A. For years, Ron Copeland of UCLA and I would play cards with The Pearl, and at some point, we would say that we had to get back to our wives. Earl would always laugh and tease us about being henpecked. And then, only about six months before last season began, we learned that he was married himself—and he'd been married all along. Peggy had been so good about letting him go out on his own that we hadn't even known that she was around. But finally she decided to put her foot down, and then it was Earl's turn to be teased about being henpecked. I spoke to Peggy on the phone and then talked to Earl, who was feeling kind of low about the game but said that things were going pretty well otherwise. He said that Peggy was hoping they would stay in Detroit in the off-season so they could settle down there, but he was still anxious to go back to Los Angeles. He knew that he would probably be offered a better off-season job in Detroit than on the Coast, but he wanted to get back to the California racetracks and swimming pools. We talked about how good it would be to lounge around the pool at my new house, and then to take off for post-time at Santa Anita. It was a little stupid, really—here it was the third week of the season and I was already dreaming of California. But that was the way losing could make you feel. It was beginning to look like a very long, cold season in Buffalo.

My spirits didn't improve much when I watched the films of the Broncos. I had seen the last part of their victory over the Jets on television, and Rich Jackson and Dave Costa, their best defensive linemen, had given Namath quite a going over. They didn't appear any less fearsome on the films. And to make matters far worse, I learned at our first meeting that Billy Shaw was going to miss the game. He had a torn muscle in his left calf and there were reports that he might miss several games. It was a pretty scary prospect. Knowing Billy, I was sure that he would recover much faster than the doctors could predict; but there was no chance that he would be ready for the Denver game. That left the task of handling Dave Costa up to a rookie named Angelo Loukas. I was by no means confident that Angelo could do the job.

Loukas was a rugged, aggressive lineman who had been born in Greece and played college ball at Northwestern. He hadn't even been selected in the draft, but he came to camp as a free agent and fought his way—literally—onto the squad. He actually hit so many people so hard and often that he instigated a number of fistfights; many veterans didn't appreciate getting belted too enthusiastically in training camp while they were still working into shape. Angelo's attitude obviously impressed the coaches and it seemed to promise him a good future. But during that week, I couldn't quite convince myself that he was a physical match for the ferocious Costa. The Oilers had messed over Loukas pretty badly in the second half when he had replaced Shaw, and even on little routine plays in practice, I noticed him getting beaten. If Costa overpowered him too severely, the Denver game figured to be very painful.

My legs felt dead in my first workouts of the week. It made me wonder if I'd failed to work myself into top shape, or if I was having trouble adjusting to Rauch's practices, which were longer than I'd been accustomed to at USC. Either way it was annoying; after two games and only twenty-nine carries, I felt as if I were dragging to the end of the season. I knew that the coach noticed, and he looked pretty disturbed. He thought I was dogging it. But when I tried to dig in harder, I just couldn't get my legs to respond. They felt as if they had weights tied to them, and the idea of going into a tough game without Billy Shaw only made the weights seem heavier.

Tom Flores left us that week. With a young prospect named Dan Darragh returning from a military obligation, Flores, who was thirty-one, was placed on waivers. The move ended one of the bleakest chapters in the history of the Bills, as well as several difficult years for Tom. Flores had been traded from Oakland to the Bills in 1967 along with veteran end Art Powell and a second-round draft choice, in exchange for Daryle Lamonica, end Glenn Bass, and two draft choices. The deal had turned into Al Davis's greatest coup, as Lamonica led the Raiders to the top of the Western Division.

As Daryle's career flourished, the deal produced rising bitterness in Buffalo. Some people around the club insisted that Powell had been a clubhouse lawyer who stirred up a lot of trouble and hurt team spirit; the older black players vehemently denied this, but the fact remained that Powell had never helped the Bills as much as they had hoped. Flores, meanwhile, underwent a nightmarish series of injuries. He was supposed to be the starting quarterback in 1967 but hurt his knee. A year later he injured a shoulder in training camp, finally got into action in midseason—and was hurt again after throwing only five passes. He had played more than our other quarterbacks during the training season, but I don't think he ever felt that he had much chance to start; Coach Rauch, after all, had been in Oakland when the decision was made to send him to Buffalo.

Tom had been one of the nicest guys in our training camp, an intelligent quarterback who could lead the team in a quiet way. I had gotten pretty angry at him once, during a brief appearance he made in the opening game; he was being rushed badly and he just turned and flipped the ball toward me with about five Jets surrounding me. I got creamed and the play could have caused a fumble, so I had a few words with him as we headed for the sidelines. But other than that, we had gotten along very well and I had a lot of respect for him. When Rauch let him go, I wished him luck—and he turned out to be as lucky as anybody else around the Bills. Len Dawson was hurt at the time, and the Kansas City Chiefs needed an extra quarterback; so Tom found not only a job, but he wound up with a winner's share of the Super Bowl loot.

As usual, something came up to distract me from total involvement with football; in midweek, I made my television acting debut. It was the show called *Medical Center* that had been taped during the summer; I played the hero, a football star named Bru Wylie who stands to lose a huge pro bonus because of a mysterious disease. The day before the show, everyone kept asking me about it. "I don't want to sit through the whole hour," Maguire said. "Tell me exactly what minute you come on and maybe I'll watch."

"I'm on for the whole show, so you'd better pay attention."

Almost all the guys did watch, and the next day they all

started calling me Bru. Somebody had even scrawled the name Bru Wylie on my practice jersey. But behind all the joking, a number of guys seemed really impressed with my acting. "O.J., I never thought I'd admit it, but you were very good," said Haven Moses. "You really fooled me." Coming from Haven, the compliment meant a lot because we were constantly putting one another down. I thought that I could have been the black Paul Newman and I still wouldn't have drawn a sincere remark from Haven.

Partly because of all the kidding about my acting, we started our Thursday practice in a pretty lackadaisical mood. Instead of firing out and hitting, we were just sort of leaning into one another. We weren't crisp, we weren't driving the way we should have been. So the coach got as mad as he'd been all year. "You're a bunch of damn patsies," Rauch said. "Why don't you ever hit some damn body? You're turning into the patsies of this league. Everybody is going to be looking forward to playing the Bills this year. They're all going to know that they can whip the Bills."

The remarks stung, and the action picked up right away. We hit as hard as we had in a long time, and I was pleased to notice that Angelo Loukas was leading the charge. Angelo was lined up against Ray Jacobs, a 280-pound veteran defensive tackle who had played for Denver and Oakland. Jacobs was imitating the moves that Dave Costa would be throwing at Loukas, and Angelo was beginning to handle them pretty well. On one play Jacobs ran right over him and clobbered me; but from that point on, Angelo seemed to pick things up. At least I knew that if he failed, it wouldn't be because he hadn't worked like hell.

The hard hitting put me in a good frame of mind. The Buffalo papers had been getting on us all week, saying pretty much what Rauch had said—that even struggling teams like Boston and Miami were anxious to get a shot at us and pick up a victory. Watching the second unit execute some plays, I said to the guys on the sidelines, "The people who are talking all that trash about us are going to be surprised. The way we're starting to hit, we're going to upset a few people."

"We've already upset a few people," said Maguire. "I hear that Ralph Wilson is upset as hell about us."

The practice field was surrounded with bystanders, as always; anybody who felt like it could wander up to a fence and see what we were doing. The spy problem had become a regular topic with us. Against Houston, we had come out in the I-formation for the first time, and their defensive men had immediately shifted into the best defense for it. Usually when you do something new, you expect to hear the defense shouting, "The I, the I," trying to make adjustments. But the Oilers hadn't said a word, and it seemed obvious that they had been expecting it. Kemp had mentioned that fact to the coach, but it was almost impossible to police that wide-open field against spies. As practice ended, a few of us looked over at the anonymous group of onlookers, wondering which one might be a spy. "If I had to guess," Maguire said, "I'd pick out that guy with the big camera and the Denver Bronco emblem on his jacket."

As worried as I was, I tried hard to build my confidence for the game. Despite their victory over the Jets, Denver did have weaknesses that I hoped we could exploit. They had two rookies playing cornerback, Bill Thompson and Grady Caveness; although they were exceptional rookies, they still figured to make some mistakes. They also had linebackers who weren't as quick as the others we'd faced; I thought we could move the ball running against them. But before we could pass over their cornerbacks or run at their linebackers, we would have to overcome their defensive line. That put tremendous pressure on our blockers, especially Loukas and our right tackle, Paul Costa.

Some of the writers seemed more concerned about Paul Costa, who would be matched against Rich Jackson, than they were about Loukas's battle with Dave Costa. Paul Costa was the most awesome physical specimen on the Bills; his 6'5" frame seemed to be covered with 250 pounds of perfectly proportioned muscle. But he had just been converted from tight end to tackle before the season and, to make things worse, he had been bothered by a bad back. Jackson was so quick that he was a threat to murder Paul if Paul's mobility was hampered. But somehow I had a feeling that Paul would do the job. He had been criticized for inconsistency, but I was sure that he would rise to the challenge of facing Jackson.

My legs still felt heavy and tired as the game approached. I hoped that a switch to lighter shoes would help, but I also wondered if the problem might be more mental than physical. I was haunted by two fears—one of Dave Costa creaming Loukas, the other of Kemp throwing away the game plan and going pass-crazy again. I knew that if we mixed up our plays and ran the ball effectively, we could keep them off balance and make things a lot easier on our pass blockers. I also hoped that they would be a little flat after the emotional peak of their Jet game. But two weeks of disappointment had cut into my natural optimism. On the eve of the game I slept restlessly, plagued by a recurrent nightmare full of desperate, incomplete passes.

Angelo Loukas was the greatest man in the world. Paul Costa's rippling muscles looked more beautiful than ever. Jack Kemp was a marvelous passer and, better yet, a brilliant signal-caller who mixed his plays with uncanny precision. The Buffalo Bills were 1-2 and only one game out of first place in the Eastern Division, and suddenly they appeared to me as a team that could do anything. Looking around that crowded, happy locker room, I kept repeating to myself, not even aware that I was talking out loud, "How sweet it is." At last, we had won a football game.

It wasn't easy. In fact, the game began as if it would be the most frustrating defeat of all. We drove to the Broncos' thirty-two-yard-line after the opening kickoff, attempted a field goal—and had it blocked. They recovered the ball, ran it all the way to our one-yard-line, and scored on the next play. "Well," I said to myself, "we're in for another of those days. We're down 7-0, and now we'll probably beat ourselves." We managed a field goal, but then Booker Edgerson was called for interference, and they completed a pass to Mike Haffner over the middle to take a 14-3 lead. I didn't know what our coverage had been on that pass, but something went wrong because Coach Rauch and safety John Pitts exchanged some angry words on the sidelines. I was afraid that we were getting ready to fall apart. But for the first time, happily, we didn't lose our composure.

Jack completed four passes, getting excellent protection; I ran a couple of sweeps, and we found ourselves with a first down at the Denver six-yard-line. Ever since I'd arrived in Buffalo, I had seen us move the ball well only to stall near the goal line. I wanted to convert this drive into a touchdown so badly I could barely think straight. On a sweep to the left, I shook off two tacklers and drove down to the three. I was confident that we could ram the ball into the end zone with a few more running plays. But Jack Kemp called a pass in the huddle. Without thinking, I said, "Oh shit." I hadn't meant to speak out loud and, being a rookie, I felt pretty stupid for criticizing our quarterback. But later, several offensive linemen came over and said that they had shared my feelings. The pass Kemp threw was almost intercepted, but Billy Masters, our tight end, saved us by knocking it out of a defender's hands.

On third down, Jack called a 28 play-pass—the play that I had hoped we would use to beat the Oilers the week before. I was supposed to fake a 28, a running play on which I block the linebacker and the fullback follows me with the ball. But instead of hitting the backer on that play, I was assigned to fake the block and slip off into the right flat for a pass. Meanwhile, Jack would fake to Wayne Patrick, our fullback, and drop back to pass. I played it well. Instead of just making a gesture toward the linebacker and rushing into the flat, I actually made contact with my man. That convinced the defensive backs that the play was a run, and really sucked them in toward the line of scrimmage. So by the time I slid off into the flat, I was wide-open, and Jack just had to loft the pass toward me. It was one of those excruciating passes that seemed to hang in the air for half an hour; it was so easy to catch that I was sure I would drop it. But it finally floated into my arms and I squeezed it so hard that nobody could have jolted it loose. We were on our way.

"Good play, that's the way to go, Jack," I told Kemp as we trotted off. If he was annoyed by what I'd said in the huddle, he didn't show it; I hoped that this one big score had drawn us all closer together. "Good calls," I added. "That's the way to lead us."

He led us strongly for the rest of the day. A field goal drew us to within a point, 14-13, and then we went ahead on a play that gave me more satisfaction than my touchdown run or my 110 yards rushing in the game. The call was for a long pass, with Haven Moses the primary receiver—and the Broncos were in a safety blitz. It seemed as if everybody might be coming, the linebackers as well as the safeties. I stayed in to pass-block, and the linebacker on my side started to come, but I sensed that he was just trying to draw me to the outside to open a path for the safety. I saw the safety start to come, so I stepped back in and I got a really good pop on him. The blitz left only one man covering Haven, and that man fell down. I thought that Haven would have beaten him in any case, but the way it turned out, he was all alone and the play went for 54 yards and a touchdown. Looking down at Tom Oberg, the safety that I had cut down, I felt as good as if I'd caught the touchdown pass myself.

It was the first time that we had enjoyed a lead at half time, and I assumed that it would make a great difference in our routine. I expected everyone to be shouting and giving pep talks to each other, with the coach giving some overall encouragement. But to my surprise, the locker room was even more businesslike than it had been when we had been losing our other games. Coach Rauch spoke to Kemp privately. The defensive guys had a special meeting of their own. Each guy on the team seemed to be getting himself up instead of depending on anyone else. And I guess that was the right way to do it because we went out and played our best quarter of the year.

Denver regained the lead shortly after half time when Al Denson, the great receiver, beat Booker Edgerson on a play very similar to the one Don Maynard had made against Booker two weeks earlier. Booker had Denson covered perfectly, but Pete Liske's pass was short, and Denson reached back and grabbed it before Booker could turn around. That put the Broncos ahead, 21-20, and I was afraid that Kemp, who had filled the air with thirty passes in the first half, would use that one-point deficit as an excuse to really go pass-crazy. This time, however,

Jack stayed with the game plan, mixing his plays beautifully to pick apart the Denver defense. We went 80 yards in eight plays—four passes and four runs—before Wayne Patrick drove over for the touchdown.

Only thirty-six seconds later, Butch Byrd stepped in front of Denson near the sideline, picked off Liske's pass, and raced into the end zone. The daring play gave us a commanding 34-21 lead, and we all surrounded Butch along the sidelines, slapping him on the shoulders and congratulating him. The loudest and most exuberant celebrant of all was Angelo Loukas—and that in itself showed just how great football can be when you're winning. I recalled one of the early training camp workouts when Angelo, battling to make the team, pulled out of the line to lead a sweep and really nailed Butch. A six-year veteran and an All-Pro who was sure of his own place on the team, Butch didn't appreciate the extra hitting, and told Loukas so. But Angelo was too wrapped up in his own struggle to worry about some veteran's anxiety about getting hurt in training camp. So he nailed Butch again and again—and finally they squared off in several angry fights. Yet here they were, a little over a month later, happily congratulating one another, each of them overjoyed that the other was doing so well. That was my idea of what football was about.

We poured it on with one more touchdown before the end of the third period, and the whole bench was alive with excitement. Billy Shaw was just hot all over, running over to us as we came off the field and saying, "That's the way to hit, that's the way to run." He must have regretted being hurt while we were enjoying such a good game, but you never would have known it from his attitude. He seemed anxious to personally keep us up, keep us going at full speed. Each time somebody made a good play, Billy was waiting to shake his hand when he reached the sideline. That was another sign of Billy's professionalism; he was determined to contribute in some way even if he couldn't go out and hit somebody for us.

With the score 41-21, Kemp jammed his right thumb and James Harris came in at quarterback. James hadn't played since the Jet game and he got a little too excited as our attack slowed down in the last quarter. I didn't help him much: I was called for holding on his very first play. Wayne Patrick was running a sweep and I got a good block on a linebacker, but I let my arms get a little too far away from my body. I didn't grab him with my hands, but my arm did get away from me and it looked as if I was holding him illegally. It was a judgment call, and it happened to go against me. I was feeling bad about it coming back to the huddle because it nullified a good run by Patrick. But Stew Barber, our veteran left tackle, made me feel better. "Did they call that on you?" he asked me. "I was holding too, but I didn't think that they saw me."

Changing quarterbacks often alters the rhythm of a team, and the switch from Kemp to Harris had an especially drastic effect. Jack called the plays in a quick and snappy cadence, while James had a slower drawl. We failed to catch his signals a few times and went in motion too quickly or mistimed our plays. The offense began to stall and Coach Rauch got furious along the sidelines. "A few touchdowns and your heads are really fat," he yelled. "I want to see you move the ball *all* the time, because you're going to be in close games when you won't be able to afford these breakdowns."

The coach was right—and unfortunately he was also prophetic—but his yelling just seemed to unsettle Harris even more. In the closing minutes we led, 41-28, and were just trying to run out the clock. But an official came over to signal the two-minute warning, and James got confused about what the official wanted and called a timeout. "Shit man," everybody yelled. "We're trying to run out the clock and you're calling timeouts."

James went to the sideline and talked to the coach. When he came back into the huddle, he said, very sheepishly, "I'm sorry, but everybody was yelling at me and I didn't know what to do."

"Oh, that's all right," said guard Joe O'Donnell. "Let's go run out that clock now." But two plays later, on a quarterback sneak, James saw a hole open. With his great competitive spirit, he couldn't resist it; instead of just shoving straight ahead to kill the remaining seconds, he broke into the open field—and ran out of bounds, stopping the clock again. All the linemen got pretty mad at that, and when he came back, they were shouting, "God damn it man, don't run out of bounds. Let's get this thing over with."

James called another quarterback sneak. Eleven seconds remained. "Do us a favor man," said Stew Barber. "Don't try and run, don't try and do anything. Just fall down on the ball so we can go home."

Joe O'Donnell had other advice for the rest of us backs: "Protect yourselves. They might be pretty mad about losing and they may come across and take some cheap shots."

We lined up, James dropped on the ball to end the game, and I saw one of their linebackers, a guy I'd nailed pretty well on a lot of running plays, start toward me. Then he stopped and a few other Broncos came over and we all said, "Good game." Maybe they wanted to prove that they could lose more gracefully than the Jets had the week before in Denver; as time had run out in that game with the Broncos ahead, the Jets had drawn about 60 yards in unsportsmanlike conduct penalties for arguing with the officials. I've never had too much to do with arguments or fights in football. In fact, whenever a tackler really sticks me, I get up and say, "Good hit." Almost invariably, the guy will answer, "That's the way to run." I don't claim that everyone should act that way, but it's always been my style and maybe it adds a little to the enjoyment of the game.

During the game, however, Rich Jackson and Dave Costa hadn't been quite as pleasant. They seemed genuinely shocked at the way Paul Costa and Angelo Loukas were whipping them, and they just cried and moaned for the whole game. Jack Kemp said that at the start of the second half Rich Jackson told him, "I took it easy on you in the first half. I'm gonna get you now." That surprised me, a younger player like Jackson needling a veteran quarterback; but it didn't matter much, because it was one of the few times Jackson got within shouting distance of Jack.

"I just stayed in front of him," Paul Costa said later. "I held him a few times early, I tripped him, I even kicked him once by accident. But after the first few series of plays there was no need to hold. He was so busy bitching that he never did get a good rush going."

Angelo Loukas had a similar explanation: "Stew Barber and I doubled up on Dave Costa on the first play and really cracked him. That seemed to set the tone. Costa's best move is to the outside, as he jerks you aside. But he never got it working too well against me. Billy Shaw and Ray Jacobs had done so much work with me all week that I felt I was ready to handle Costa." I guess everyone in the locker room could have given similar descriptions of the game. In our earlier games, we had been a group of individuals playing our own games. This time everybody had been thinking of the other guys. On our sweeps, the wide receivers cracked back and wiped defenders out of the plays. Our linemen were really driving into their targets, and the backs were cracking the linebackers. And Kemp played one of his finest games. In fact, Denver coach Lou Saban—the former Buffalo coach from the championship years—was quoted as saying, "The rest we expected. The difference was Kemp. Hats off to the man."

Butch Byrd and Booker Edgerson were among the few quiet players in the locker room—partly because they were too tired to do much yelling. "How many passes did Denver throw?" asked Booker. "Must have been a hell of a lot."

"Liske threw forty-five passes," he was told.

"We threw a hell of a lot, too," said Butch. We had thrown forty-two.

"Yeah, a lot of them when we could have been killing the clock," said Booker. But the complaining was only half-serious, a reflection of their exhaustion. "Don't forget," said Booker, "the Broncos were alternating their receivers. Nobody was alternating us. That makes it a long afternoon."

Personally, I was delighted with my game. I totalled 110 yards on twenty-four carries, and I had averaged seven or eight yards a carry until late in the game when we were killing the clock with short-yardage traps. I also caught five passes for 25 yards, but by far the most satisfying aspect of the game was my blocking. I really nailed the linebackers on our off-tackle plays and sweeps, and I cut down several blitzers while I was pass-blocking. Twice I even noticed the linebackers lining up unusually far outside to avoid getting hooked in by the blockers— and I still managed to stick them and help set up big gains. After a career spent doing very little except running with the ball, I was just learning that it could also be a lot of fun to block.

Coach Rauch met us at the dressing room door to congratulate us. When we were all inside, he said, "Let's get down on our knees and thank the Lord." We all knelt in silence for about thirty seconds, and then he said, "You had a good game. You went after people. We had some mistakes, but there was nothing we can't work on and correct." Everybody in the room felt the same way. A cynic might have pointed out that we had merely beaten a team that was operating without its first-string quarterback, Steve Tensi, and its best runner, Floyd Little. But nobody listens to cynics on a team that has just broken out of a long and futile slump. We were victors, we were suddenly in contention again, and best of all, we were beginning to feel like a team. For the Bills, football became fun again that afternoon.

Chapter Ten

Personal Wars

After the Denver game, I enjoyed a day off—my first since reporting to the Bills. At last, I found myself with a Monday all to myself; there were no commercials to film, speeches to make, or appointments to keep. I slept late and then took my time reading the papers, savoring every word about our victory. The writers who had been wondering if we would ever win a game were suddenly talking about a playoff spot—and the players were beginning to think along the same lines. The Eastern Division race was a jumble: Houston led with a 2-1 record and we were tied with the Jets at 1-2. Despite our poor start we were still in the middle of the race, and more important, we had another shot at the Oilers that week in the Astrodome. It was the first game that could be called crucial for us, and I was convinced that we could erase most of the mistakes of our first Oiler game and whip them. If we did, we would be tied for the division lead and in a good position to finish first or second and make the post-season playoffs.

After relaxing around the house for most of the day, I drove downtown to the Bills' office to sort out some personal appearance requests with Jack Horrigan, the head of public relations. Those requests never stopped piling up during the season. They came from booster groups, boys clubs, and countless charities, and almost all were worthwhile—but there were just too many to handle. Horrigan, a quietly efficient executive, devoted many hours during the season to helping me straighten out my schedule. Without Jack, in fact, I hate to think of the number of engagements I might have forgotten; I could have ended the season with a bad reputation as a no-show. At USC, my idea of good public relations was simply to be myself and cooperate with the writers and fans. As with so many other aspects of my life, public relations became much more complicated in Buffalo. I was lucky to have Horrigan around.

Before we began the week's work on Tuesday, we had a full-scale team meeting, presided over by Harry Jacobs. As the defensive captain, Harry was an acknowledged leader, and he tried to influence the team in a number of ways. First, he was a proud and hard-working player. Like Billy Shaw, he practiced as hard as he played and he never allowed himself to let down. Harry was thirty-two and some observers had written that he was slowing down, but he still made up for any physical shortcomings with his keen football mind and his hustle. You couldn't help but respect him for it.

In addition, Harry was a very religious man, a leader in the Fellowship of Christian Athletes. He had set up a program of optional Sunday chapel sessions before our pre-game meals, and he loved to talk to the guys about religion and inspiration. Because he was so sincere and straightforward, the players accepted a lot of comments from him that would have been considered very corny coming from anyone else. But Harry had a habit of getting carried away when he started making a speech. It would take him ten minutes to say what somebody else might express in a few sentences, and his listeners would start getting restless.

At the meeting, Harry spoke about the game ball. Everyone was happy with the idea of just having a winning game ball to give away, but Harry went on so long about our alternatives that some of the guys got pretty impatient. He said we could give either one ball or two—for offense and defense—and we could decide whom to give it to either right after the game or after viewing the films. He went on about the pros and cons of each method, and a few of the other players commented on the issue, but we finally just dropped the subject without making a decision and gave that first game ball to Coach Rauch. "I appreciate it," the coach told us. "I think this game gave us a lift that we really needed. I'm sorry I got so mad during the fourth quarter, but I hated to see you losing your composure because we won't be able to afford that in a close ball game. I hope we can really get going now and eliminate some of our mistakes. Now let's look at the game films."

The films did show a number of errors and Coach Rauch naturally commented on them, but overall the Denver game was satisfying to watch. And I was even happier when I noticed that our offensive film session lasted longer than the one for the defense. In our earlier games, the defense had been on the field so much that their films ran about ten or fifteen minutes longer. This time, for once, we could feel that the offense had done its share. After the meetings, we had a lively workout in sweats. The tension of preparing for our first truly big game seemed to hang in the air, and I felt invigorated.

Ben Gregory had driven me to practice that day, and as usual, he was dressed and ready to go home long before I was. "Come on, man," he kept saying, "I'm going to leave

O.J. makes his first appearance before the Buffalo fans.
(*Photo by Robert L. Smith*)

On the sidelines with Coach Rauch . . .
(Photo by Robert L. Smith)

. . . and teammates. No. 55 is Paul Maguire. *(Photo by Robert L. Smith)*

Running into traffic: against the Jets. *(Photo by Robert L. Smith)*

Following a blocker with a screen pass. *(Photo by Robert L. Smith)*

Passing a training camp physical.
(SPORTS ILLUSTRATED *photo*
by Neil Leifer, © Time Inc.)

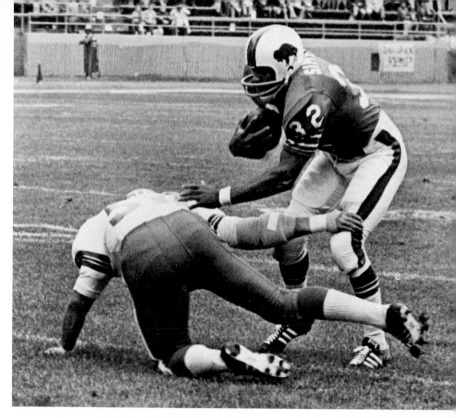

In the victory over Denver. *(Photo by Robert L. Smith)*

Even a long season has its bright spots.
(SPORTS ILLUSTRATED *photo by Neil Leifer,* © *Time Inc.*)

you here if you don't hurry." Ben was always in a hurry, even though we had no place special to go. It was just a sign of his own nervous energy; his injured knee was coming along slowly, and he was getting very impatient about returning to action. On that day he seemed even more on edge than he had been earlier, and when we finally got into his car, I asked him about it. "I am getting pretty restless," he said. "When it looked like we were just going to lose and lose, it didn't seem quite as bad to watch from the sidelines. But now we look like we can do some winning. We have a young team and it's going to get better. I can't wait to get back into the middle of it." I felt sorry for Ben, but his attitude reflected a healthy change in the mood of the whole team. We were all starting to believe in ourselves.

Jack Kemp's mother died that week, and Jack flew home to California. That cast a pall over the beginning of our Wednesday practice. Everybody felt very bad about Jack and wondered when he would come back. I tried to put myself in his place, and I thought that it would be very hard to play a football game a few days after a shock such as that. But I guess true professionals don't think that way. I learned that Jack planned to be back the next day.

Maybe the coach wanted to snap us out of our doldrums, or maybe he thought that our first victory had made us a little too cocky; in any case, he put us through our hardest workout since the end of the double sessions in training camp. It was supposed to be defensive day, but we get a hell of a workout on offense, too. Coach Rauch always likes to see about five minutes of offensive work at the end of defensive day—but that day he got carried away with himself. The five minutes stretched to a half-hour as he kept calling, "One more . . . one more." After running countless plays for the defense to work on, we were really dragging during those extra offensive plays. Each time the coach said "one more," it actually meant two or three more, and it felt like the session would never end. After one play, center Al Bemiller said, "I didn't know how good I had it when Lou Saban was here."

"When Saban was here you were winning," I said. "I guess those championships made hard workouts seem a lot easier." I was sure that once we started winning a lot of games, we'd all feel better about the practices. But running what seemed to be my fiftieth 28-trap play in a row, I also wondered how somebody as bright as Coach Rauch could have so much trouble keeping track of the time.

Kemp returned on Thursday. Not knowing exactly what to say, I avoided speaking to him during our first pass-pattern drill. Then we found ourselves on the sideline together and Jack mentioned, "Boy, it was really smoggy on the Coast."

"I'm very sorry you had to go out there for that reason," I told him. "But I hope things didn't go too badly."

"The L.A. area is really excited about football," he said, anxious to change the subject. "USC, UCLA, and the Rams are all undefeated."

"Yeah, everybody's undefeated this year."

"Well, not everybody. Occidental lost a game."

Jack had played at Occidental, a small school in southern California, and he loved to include it among the football powers whenever we talked. Hearing him kid about it, I was glad that he was taking things so well.

I could see the coach getting annoyed at me again as practice wore on. My legs were dead, and I felt two knots that seemed ready to pull loose at any moment; I knew that I looked as if I were dragging. Jack suggested that I ask to be excused from the wind sprints after practice, and I was tempted. But maybe the coach was reading our minds, because at the end of practice, he sent us in without any wind sprints. The next day we had a light workout, and on Saturday, we left for Houston. My legs began to feel better, and my mood was optimistic. I no longer felt as if I were exploring, searching for my place. In fact, I no longer felt like a rookie. I was a full-fledged member of a team that was facing its greatest challenge of the season.

As the Oiler game approached, I looked around at my teammates, trying to understand just what a big game—and a football season—meant to them. There were fringe players trying to hang on with the Bills, veterans trying to climb back to the top, and young players like me trying to prove themselves. In some ways we were moving closer together, but in other areas we remained apart, separated by our ages and attitudes. It occurred to me that the Bills were not only a team, but a group of individuals fighting grim personal wars. In college football, team spirit had seemed to be a simple, single-minded dedication. Among the pros, motivation was a more complex, personal matter—a matter that continued to fascinate me as the season progressed.

Coach Rauch himself was waging one of the most intense individual battles. He had the best coaching record in pro football, but he had lived for years with the hints that he was merely a figurehead following Al Davis's orders in Oakland. To prove what he could do without front-office "help" or "interference"—depending on the point of view—he had accepted the challenge of rebuilding a 1-12-1 club in Buffalo. His desire to have complete control over the Bills' fate was evident in almost everything he did. In practices, he was on top of everything that went on, trying to imprint his system and his personality on each of our actions. He felt strongly that a head coach should be deeply and directly involved in teaching his team, instead of merely coordinating a group of assistants as some coaches did. This was reflected in his choice of assistants—bright but relatively inexperienced men who occasionally seemed as unfamiliar with the system as the players were. Some of the veterans commented often on the assistants, who were apparently much less experienced than Buffalo coaches of past years. But it seemed that the coach wanted it that way so everyone would be sure to do things his way. There was no doubt that he was in complete charge—and that he was willing to take all blame as well as credit for whatever happened to the Bills. I admired him for placing all that pressure on himself. And I was certain that he would eventually enjoy a lot of credit for building a new, powerful Buffalo team.

Jack Kemp was fighting a war of his own, to prove that the many people who said he was washed up were wrong. Jack was coming back from a broken leg that had kept him out of the entire 1968 season. Many people said that, at thirty-four, he should have retired on the laurels he had gathered in the Bills' title years. During our preseason games and our first two losses, a lot of writers had been pretty rough on Jack. After his great performance against Denver, the same writers were quick to praise him, but he knew that people would jump on him again the minute he faltered. There were doubters among the players, too. Some wondered openly if Jack was more interested in his stock dealings, politics, and plans for the future than he was in football; others claimed that Jack was too statistic-conscious.

At times, when we abandoned game plans and went pass-crazy, I also wondered if he was too worried about his statistics. But then I would talk to Jack in practice or in the locker room, and I'd know that whatever he was doing, he was doing it for the team. Jack was thirty-four, but when he talked football he acted like a young kid, excited and in love with the game. I refused to accept the idea that he was just trying to prove something for himself. He was playing for the team, and even when I got upset with his play-calling, I reminded myself that he was a proud veteran of some great years. I was rooting for him to win his own battle and lead us to the top again.

Al Bemiller, the center, was involved in an unusual personal struggle of his own. Al was a steady thirty-year-old veteran who had started every game for the Bills since 1961. He had never made All-Pro, partly because Jim Otto of Oakland was an automatic choice at that position every year, but he was a solid, experienced man. And last fall he attempted to translate his long career with the Bills into political success by running for supervisor of his hometown, a Buffalo suburb called Cheektowaga. I was surprised when I heard about his campaign; if I had been asked to pick out a future town supervisor or mayor on the Bills, I would have suggested a speechmaker like Harry Jacobs. Al was a more subdued type; he was such a hard worker that I thought he would be a good office-holder, but I wasn't sure if he would be flashy enough to be a good campaigner. He said that he was a decided underdog in the election, but we all hoped that he would make a good run for it—and that a Bills winning streak might give him a boost.

Al's campaign raised a number of questions in my mind. Was he just playing football so he could further his political career? Would he retire if he won the election? Was it detracting from his concentration on winning? Actually, I assumed that Al had answered those questions for himself. But that wasn't what bothered me.

The same kind of questions applied to Jack Kemp and his stocks and politics, to many other Bills—and especially to O.J. Simpson, who was involved in more outside activities than anyone else. I tried to sort out the meanings of my own personal wars, on and off the field—and my situation was as hard to understand as any on the Bills.

A few games had already proven what most intelligent observers had predicted—that I wasn't going to simply run over everybody I faced in the pros. But I still felt that I could have a great rookie season and prove some things to my detractors. Before the Denver game, Floyd Little had told reporters that he knew what I was going through because he had averaged only 2.9 yards per carry during his own rookie year. He said that I shouldn't worry because it would take me a couple of years to get going. I disagreed. I was sure that I would improve over the years, but I also felt that I could be a very good football player right away.

Off the field, my business interests were flourishing. I was on the phone almost every day with Chuck Barnes in Indianapolis and his brother Bruce in Los Angeles, learning about the investments they were making and the contracts they were negotiating. Before I left for Houston, Bruce called with the first report on an oil stock we had invested in—and the profits were phenomenal. In addition to the profits, I enjoyed the idea of turning to the financial page once in a while to check on some of my stocks. It gave me a feeling of maturity and self-assurance—a sense of widening my horizons beyond football.

I knew that there was criticism of my extensive outside interests, however, and I honestly wasn't sure how justified it was. Up to that point, it had all been a dizzy, thrilling roller coaster ride, a dazzling experience in high finance for a ghetto kid who hadn't been able to afford a letter-jersey during high school. But now I was trying to pause and get things into balance. A lot of people had told me, sometimes with a hint of sarcasm, "You don't even need to play football any more." That jolted me, because I'd always needed football—not from a financial point of view, just from a basic need. I needed the thrill and contact and challenge of the game, and I also needed to be respected for doing something special. Football had gained me that respect, and I wasn't ready to conclude that I no longer needed it.

One night I hung up after a long conversation with Chuck concerning some off-season commitments, and found myself wondering if I would still have enough time to do a movie if a good acting offer came along. I stopped myself abruptly. Here it was the first month of the football season, and I was trying to make room among my endorsement plans for a movie. I suddenly realized that I would have to readjust my thinking. I had to look at myself as a football player first and a businessman second. The business would have to remain with Chuck and Bruce, while I gave full attention to football. Once I had been in the AFL for a while, maybe I could devote more time to other things without hurting my play. But I was a rookie and I was determined to live up to what people expected from me. To do that, I would have to shove business to the back of my mind and concentrate on becoming a great pro football player. That was my personal war.

On a team engaged in so many personal struggles, it was inevitable that there would be some clashes. It was no secret in Buffalo that Rauch and Kemp had argued over Kemp's failure to follow the game plans; the rest of us had also had our disagreements. But unity cannot be forced on a group of professionals; it has to be developed slowly. And gradually I felt that a lot of us were coming together, sometimes in subtle and unusual ways. James Harris, for example, was laboring under the great pressure of trying to become the first successful black quarterback. Early in camp, he had been very shy about taking charge of the offense, and in the Denver game he had suffered through those embarrassing mistakes. Yet he was beginning to fit in and gain confidence, off the field as well as on it. He was spending a lot of time with Marlin Briscoe, a proud, outgoing guy who had quarterbacked at Denver the year before, and some of Marlin the Magician's brash confidence was rubbing off. At the card games and bull sessions around our apartment building, James was beginning to act like a future leader.

Willie Grate, a reserve tight end who came to us from Houston, also began to fit into our group—although I couldn't take much credit for that. Willie, like Robert James, was a shy, retiring southern black, and I teased him quite a bit. Watching films of our special teams after the Denver game, I saw that Willie missed every block he tried. I started saying, "Look at Willie, fellas," and when the film showed him missing another block, everybody laughed at him. It was the kind of kidding everyone expected at USC, but again, I found that pros take those things more seriously. When we left the meeting, Willie told me, "From now on I'll just call you 'Cheese,' because you're such a big cheese around here." I looked at him and saw that he was really hurt. I decided to start being more careful about my wisecracks, and I hoped that Willie would have a great game against his old teammates in Houston.

I was close to Bubba Thornton from the beginning of training, although some people may have thought we were an unlikely match. Bubba was a rookie wide receiver from Texas Christian, and he talked with a slow drawl he picked up in some little town in Texas where he was born.

He turned out to be one of the nicest guys on the Bills. He was also funny to be around because he was just an old country boy learning about the North. One night, Marquerite and I decided to show Bubba something new and took him and his wife up to Niagara Falls for some Chinese food—which they had never even tried. Being from San Francisco, we naturally considered ourselves experts on the subject, and when we sat down I said, "Leave everything to me. I'll order a bunch of specialties and you'll love them." I ordered some lavish seven-course feast, and when it arrived, I didn't even recognize most of the food. Bubba tried to act like it was fine, but we all just toyed with it. We ate only about a fifth of what they served. Finally Bubba asked, "What is this stuff called, anyway? Ho Chi Minh?" All the way home, he laughed about how glad he was not to live in San Francisco where people eat that Ho Chi Minh all the time. When we got back to Buffalo, we all stopped for hamburgers.

As the weeks passed and I grew closer to a number of the younger Bills, I gradually ceased to miss the close friendships we had all made at USC. I knew that in the long run I would play more years with the Bills than I had at any one place before, and I began to look ahead to a lot of good, lasting relationships. I hoped that soon we would be bound together as tightly as the championship Buffalo teams had been—and I was sure that a big victory over Houston would take us a long way in that direction.

Getting ready for my first game on Astroturf, I called a representative of the Adidas shoe company in Los Angeles. I had always worn Adidas football shoes; in fact, before they made a football shoe, I had worn their soccer shoes because they were so light. The Adidas man was anxious to know if I had enough shoes, and he mentioned that they had a new shoe made specially for Astroturf—

but he said he didn't have any ready for me yet. Then he casually asked if anyone else had contacted me about shoes.

"Yes," I said. "Somebody from Puma talked to me about a shoe for Astroturf."

I knew, of course, that I would shock him with that statement. Adidas and Puma are the two German-based companies that monopolize most track-shoe manufacturing. They are run by two brothers who hate one another and compete furiously. Neither company had moved too far into sports outside of track in this country, but both hoped to, and I knew how fiercely they competed from my days in track and field. After a minute of nervous silence, the Adidas guy said, "I'll fly to Houston to bring you our Astroturf shoes. And I'd like to talk to you about endorsing Adidas shoes."

I couldn't help laughing at the fast action I got just by mentioning Puma. But I was a little annoyed with myself again: Here I was going into another game thinking about possible endorsements instead of simple football. On the way to Houston I talked to Robert James and James Harris, and both of them were worried about their money problems. Naturally, they said, "You're so lucky, O.J., not to have to worry about money." I agreed that I was lucky, but there were moments—like that one—when I wished that I could be like Robert James or James Harris, with all my cares and challenges taking shape solely on the football field.

The Astrodome was like something from outer space. We practiced in it on the afternoon before the game, and it was as quiet as a giant tomb. A woman was directing guided tours somewhere up in the highest tiers, and her voice echoed down through the pastel levels and reverberated over us in a shrill, eerie way. Each time the ball slapped against someone's hand or foot, the staccato sound would bounce back to us from the far reaches of the huge dome. Gradually the tourists worked their way down into the lower seats, listening to the amplified voice of the guide reciting statistics—the height, weight, and size of just about every piece of metal in the building. Working out in our raggedy red and blue sweats down at the bottom of the building, I guess we seemed a very insignificant part of the tour's attraction. Then Maguire drew the attention of the sightseers by booming some punts right into their midst. A few women yelled with fright and we all broke up and got back down to earth.

In a real sense, it was the Astroturf, not the Dome, that scared me. I had never played on it, but from watching games on it, I had gotten the idea that it was an artificial rug with some fairly thick padding underneath. That was true of synthetic turf on some outdoor stadiums, but not of the Astroturf. It was just laid down on a hard dirt surface, and it felt like a covered cement floor. The Adidas representative showed up with the new shoes, and I felt that my traction was very good; but I still felt strange on that hard surface.

Two other little things bothered me. First, I noticed that the Astrodome field was perfectly flat, instead of being crowned like most fields. On a typical football field, the middle is higher than the sides; it's something you hardly think about, until you have to play on a flat field. I think that many quarterbacks have slight difficulty adjusting to it and tend to throw the ball a little lower than they intend. In addition, I was worried about the lights; in our workout I lost a couple of passes. But I assumed that there would be more lighting for the game and decided to stop letting such small things bug me.

The Astrodome lighting was fine during the game— but my own lights went out in the third period. I caught a pass in traffic, got hit hard, and flipped over backwards, slamming my head against that hard turf. I only missed a few plays, but the headache stayed with me all day. And the events on the field didn't help it at all. The game was a nightmare. The breaks, the calls by the officials, and our own mistakes all went against us. But the real reason that our hopes for a big win slipped away was simply that we got whipped in almost every department. Pete Beathard had a terrible afternoon for the Oilers, completing only ten of twenty-eight passes and getting three intercepted by Butch Byrd. But we didn't fare any better and wound up losing, 28-14, in another game that I honestly felt we could have won.

Once again our defense played better than Houston's 28 points would make it seem. Jerry Levias kept us in the hole for much of the game with great kickoff and punt returns, and we gave up the ball on three fumbles and three interceptions. Yet the defense tried valiantly to keep us within range—and even turned in one of our most successful offensive plays of the game. We were down, 7-0, with a fourth down on the Houston forty-four, and Maguire went in to punt. The whole crowd seemed to gasp as Paul threw the first pass of his ten-year career, and completed it for 19 yards to Robert James. Maguire came to the bench chortling and howling, "I'm ready to go in at quarterback now, coach." We were all shouting and clapping Paul and Robert on their shoulders, and as I went back onto the field, I had the feeling that old Maguire had come through and given us just the spark we needed.

On the next play Wayne Patrick fumbled and the threat was dead. On that afternoon, no spark seemed to be enough to help us.

Wayne Patrick had a disastrous day. He got his hands on the ball only four times—and fumbled it three times.

One of the fumbles came on a terrible call. He barely grabbed a pass and dropped it as he got hit; everyone was sure that it was an incompletion except the ref, who called it a completion and fumble, and gave the ball over to Houston. Patrick, who was nicknamed Wingate for some reason nobody seemed to know, was an easygoing, hardworking guy who had struggled to win the fullback job from Bill Enyart. After his third fumble, the coach replaced him with Enyart. I felt very sorry for Wingate, but was surprised to see him looking fairly calm on the bench. He was just that type. He seemed able to smile through anything.

I had my worst rushing game, managing only 27 yards in thirteen tries. Our offensive line wasn't exactly opening huge holes for me, but I wasn't doing any good running either. I was stutter-stepping, trying to find running room and break away—and as a result, I was giving Houston's quick linemen good shots at me. I should have been hitting the holes crisply, trying to salvage whatever yardage I could out of each play. It was just another small lesson in the technique of pro ball, and as always, the learning was painful.

Even with all our problems, we were in the game for most of the afternoon. Trailing by 14-0, we had the ball near midfield when Kemp threw a soft sideline pass toward Bubba Thornton, and Kenny Houston, the Oilers' safety, intercepted it and ran it all the way. The play should have broken our spirit once and for all, but I noticed one thing striking about it. Billy Shaw, who had been pass-blocking and happened to be closest to Houston as he ran, lumbered after Houston as if his life depended on it. Everyone knew Billy could never catch up to a fast safety-man, of course. But the effort was typical of him.

Bubba returned the next kickoff 51 yards, Marlin Briscoe made several good catches, and Max Anderson scored as I watched from the bench, trying to get my head back together after my injury. I went back in on our next series, again thinking that we could come back. But as happened so often to us, we got within range only to let our last chance slip away. Some Oiler penalties helped us to a first down on their seven-yard-line, and on our first try I ran to the one. On second down I hoped we would blast straight ahead; maybe I could just hurdle over the pile for the touchdown. But instead we tried another off-tackle play, and they closed the hole and tripped me up for a yard loss. On third-and-two, the coach sent Max Anderson in for me, carrying a pass play. Max was the primary receiver, but he was well covered, and before Jack could find another target, he was nailed for a 5-yard loss. Then we tried a final desperate pass, but Haven Moses had trouble eluding Miller Farr and running his pattern, and Jack's pass fell harmlessly in the end zone. That seemed to take the heart out of our defense because Houston immediately put together its only real drive of the day to open a 28-7 lead and bury us.

Everybody on the bench was furious after we blew that goal-line chance, and everybody was still mad in the locker room. I was madder than anybody, not only about the result but about my own condition. During the last part of the game I had been alarmed when I looked at some of the numbers and names on guys' uniforms—and couldn't make them out. My vision was badly blurred, my head ached like hell, and my mood was really vile. One of the guys said something about how we should have run the ball over the goal, and how we blew our chances. "It's getting to be the same story all the time," I snapped. "We all bitch on the sidelines and try to blame somebody for it, but the fact is we're just getting our ass kicked."

Talking quietly to reporters, Coach Rauch did his best

to control his emotions. "It's a matter of confidence," he said. "With a second down on their one, you should get the ball over. It's disheartening to lose games like this, because we're at the point now where we can start winning some games." Staring across the room at a blurred scene full of angry athletes hurriedly getting dressed, I could only hope that he was right.

Chapter Eleven

Hell of a Headache

The ride home from Houston was the most miserable of my life. The Houston airport is a million miles from town: the bus ride out there probably took forty-five minutes, but it seemed endless. The trainer had given me some medication for my head, but it was slow in taking effect and I felt awful. At the airport, we were told that the plane couldn't leave the ground for another hour. Most of the guys wandered around the airport area, but I got right on the plane. I took the arm rests out of the seats and stretched out to try to sleep. It seemed unbelievable that I could be feeling so bad. I had played a bad game individually, the team had had a bad day—and now my head was throbbing and my vision clouded.

Gradually I slipped off into a half-sleep, a kind of dim twilight. My eyes were closed and my mind halfway into deep sleep, but I could still hear the voices of my teammates as they filtered into the plane. The engines finally roared and I felt us lift off the ground; from behind me, the voices barely penetrated my awareness. Jack Kemp was explaining to John Pitts about how the stock market works. Four or five of the guys were starting a card game.

A few others were laughing about some stuff they'd seen in the terminal. I felt puzzled and a little annoyed. At USC, when we lost a game, there could be nothing funny. All the next week, we'd work extra hard to make up for it; it would never leave our minds. Now the Bills had not only lost a game, but possibly lost their best chance of the season to get into contention—and the guys were taking it in stride. I guess the attitude could be called a professional one: "Well, that one's behind us and we've got to play next week's game, so what's the use of worrying." But in that area I was very much a rookie because I couldn't develop that casual attitude. I felt bad about losing. I felt bad about the way we lost. I thought the coach could have done some things differently, and I knew that most of the guys agreed with me. I had hoped that some of the older guys would get mad enough to discuss some things with Kemp and Coach Rauch. But then I heard them all laughing and getting their minds off the game, and I realized that nobody was going to say anything. I wondered if the whole season was going to be just as frustrating.

About halfway home I woke up and felt a little better. Chuck DeVleigher, a rookie defensive lineman, sat near me and we talked about my hopes for a movie career and about movies in general. We laughed and joked a little, and I began to push the game toward the back of my mind. It was a strange scene. In training camp, I had picked out DeVleigher as one guy who definitely didn't like me, and I sure didn't like him much. We had exchanged a few angry words, and I had been certain that we'd never get along. But on that dreary trip, I learned that he was a good guy. That was the way things were supposed to be on a team—win or lose. Eventually you had to develop a strong bond with your teammates. They were your friends, they were men you'd have to depend upon, and they were people you'd be spending years with. At USC, I would have done anything for my teammates and they would have done anything for me. Talking to DeVleigher, I hoped that we would all eventually feel the same way in Buffalo. At least that feeling seemed to be growing.

I slept for most of the day after the game, figuring that my headache would go away. But I just couldn't shake it, and by night I was dreading the next day's workout. The doctors had said something about doing some tests on my head, and I wondered if I'd have to go through that later in the week.

I was surprised to see that the AP named George Webster as Lineman of the Week. The story said that George "held O.J. to 27 yards." But I had actually run very few plays or patterns into his area. It was one of those cases in which the writers wanted to credit somebody with doing the job on me, so they chose the best-known member of the Oiler defense. The guys who really gave me trouble in the game were the defensive linemen, especially end Elvin Bethea. In fact, Bethea was all over me during both of our games with Houston. The first time he hit me in the Dome, I said, "Oh no, not you again."

"Yeah, it's me," he said, "and wherever you go, I'm going to be right with you all day." He was right. Our biggest problem against Houston was that we couldn't get the end man on their line. On a sweep, if somebody can cut that end down, we can open things up. But if he fights his way along the line, it makes it tough for our pulling guards to turn upfield, and it makes it very hard for me to find a hole. Bethea did a great job of sliding down that line. It seemed as if he was always on his feet.

The next morning, Coach Rauch saw that I was still pretty low about our loss. 'You're going to lose them," he said. "You're going to take your knocks, but you just have to keep coming back. You just have to pick up where you left off and keep driving." I understood what he meant. In pro ball, you play so much that you've got to expect to lose some of the time. You've got to forget it and worry about your next opponent. But it still wasn't easy.

Booker Edgerson addressed a team meeting that day to tell us about a cocktail party that the black businessmen in the area were giving for the team. "It's the first time the black community has held this kind of affair," he said, "and I hope that all of us, black and white, can be there to show our support." I had heard about the party, but I hadn't planned to be there. It was scheduled for the following Sunday, after our Saturday night game with Boston; I had hoped to go to Pittsburgh on that day to see Mike Taylor, my USC friend who was an offensive tackle with the Steelers. In addition, I had been annoyed by some guy who had called me to announce the party. He had expressed it as an ultimatum—you be there for the black brothers or else—and so I'd decided not to go along with him. But when Booker spoke about it, I realized that it was my duty to go. These were black people trying to do something for the team and for the community, and it would look pretty bad if the white guys showed up to help the racial situation in town, while some black players stayed away. Regardless of the way I felt about the guy who had called me, I told Booker I would definitely be there.

It was unusual to see Booker taking charge of a meeting that way; he wasn't known for saying too much to the group. I was just getting to know Booker, and he was one of the most interesting members of the team. In high school and college, Booker had been a top athlete in track, baseball, and basketball as well as football, but he had attended a small school, Western Illinois, and hadn't gotten much credit. He signed with the Bills as a free agent in 1962, and became one of the most talented and least appreciated cornerbacks in the league. Booker had a deceptively cool approach to everything he did, including football. If he lost money in a card game, he would never moan and groan the way some guys did. "There'll be plenty more games," was his attitude. On any other issue he discussed, he would be just as casual. And in practice, he showed the same traits. He would run hard with a receiver, make sure his man was completely covered, and then just let the ball sail by him. As long as he knew his man was covered, Booker didn't feel that he had to prove anything by making fancy catches in practice.

In games, he was one of the steadiest of defensive backs, but he wasn't noticed too much because he would seldom gamble to try for an interception. Booker's style was just to go out every week and match his man step for step, trying to bat every pass down. If an occasional pass got away from him—such as the circus catches Don Maynard and Al Denson had already made against him for touchdowns—he would just trot back to his position and get ready to stop the next one. Before and during a game, he was expressionless. Others might be talking, yelling, or milling around, but Booker would be by himself, looking about as worried as if he were going out for an afternoon walk. Once I was teasing him about having to cover great receivers such as Maynard or Lance Alworth. "It don't matter whether a guy's name is Lance or Joe Blow," he said. "I don't even look to see if the number on his back is nineteen or zero. Anybody on that field can beat you—and anybody on that field can be covered." Before a game, Booker didn't even bother to warm up much. He knew when he was ready—and I think most AFL receivers knew, too. Some people insisted that he was the most underrated cornerback in the league.

Booker and Butch Byrd, our other cornerback, made an

interesting pair. They were both quiet around the locker room, but away from football they were very different. Booker liked to run around and be in the middle of the action all the time, while Butch was more of a reserved family man. Both were loners in a sense. Playing cornerback can make you a loner because you're always out there by yourself, under tremendous pressure. As Lem Barney of Detroit, perhaps the best of all cornerbacks, once said, "It's the lonesomest place in town."

Butch's style was also in sharp contrast to Booker's. Butch was an all-out, hell-for-leather hustler, one of the most aggressive defensive backs around. He'd always gamble for the interception, and sometimes he would lose and leave his man wide-open. His three interceptions off Beathard in Houston had put him into the league lead, but he had also been burned more often than Booker. I thought that both men gained certain advantages from their styles of play. Booker gave up very few touchdown passes and, for that matter, remarkably few passes of any kind. But Butch, by his reckless gambling, could intimidate quarterbacks. Joe Namath, for one, hated to throw toward George Sauer when Butch was on George because one slip could mean an interception. Booker was thirty and Butch was twenty-eight. Watching them on the field and talking to them off it, I hoped that their careers would go on for a long time.

With a 1-3 record, I knew that Coach Rauch might be making some changes. The first were two releases: He cut DeVleigher, the tackle whom I had just started to know on our trip home from Houston, and Monte Ledbetter, a wide receiver. DeVleigher didn't seem to take it too hard. He was hard to faze anyway, and instead of cutting him, they sent him to a Continental League team—so it seemed as if they had some hope for him. Ledbetter was a likeable, colorful guy who had always been chewing on a big hunk of tobacco. He had played in many of our card games, and a lot of the players hated to see him go. But it appeared that he had made a mistake that brought it on himself.

Monte had gone to Rauch, according to reports, and said, "Coach, I know I'm not going to play unless somebody gets hurt."

"I know that, too," said the coach.

"Then either play me, trade me, or let me go."

Monte got the third choice—his release. No one knew if he would have been cut anyway, but all the veterans were joking about how he had rushed things and cost himself money. If he had waited another day and practiced on Wednesday, they would have paid him right through the week's game. By getting cut on Tuesday, he blew the game check. Some of the guys who'd played cards with him mentioned that it was typical of Monte's luck.

Another player worried about what changes might be made was Wayne Patrick. To make up for those three fumbles in Houston, Wingate practiced as if he were in the Super Bowl. All season long he'd been battling Enyart for the fullback spot, and some people thought he'd lost it for good in Houston. But the coach was pretty disillusioned with Enyart, too. When I had arrived at camp, I had heard Enyart was too slow to be a pro fullback and would probably end up at linebacker. For a while, Bill surprised everybody with his speed, takeoff, and overall quickness; but then he had begun to tail off. He seemed a little unsure of himself, taking a few strides to get going and find the hole instead of snapping right into it. I was pretty sure that the coach was going to go back to Wingate—but Wingate was taking no chances. Even though we had a routine workout in sweats, he really cracked into the holes.

Watching films of the Boston Patriots, I began to shake

off my bad mood. They were one team that I was dead
sure we could run on. They had two defensive linemen
that were really strange looking—Jim Hunt and Houston
Antwine. They were both short, six feet tall or less, and
they weighed about 285 each. They were quick as cats,
too. But overall, I got the impression that we could move
the ball on the ground against them more easily than we
had against anyone else. And after that 27-yard debacle
against the Oilers, I wanted a big game so badly I could
taste it.

In fact, our whole offense needed a lift, as Jim Peters
pointed out in the *Buffalo Courier-Express*. Peters, in addition to several other writers, really got down on our offensive line. He said that our linemen were old and tired
and that they didn't want to block for me and the other
backs. The only guy on the line that showed anyone he
really wanted to hit, according to the articles, was Angelo
Loukas, I agreed that Angelo was a pleasure to play with.
He made mistakes, but he always went at it about 110
percent. But I didn't think it was fair to blame just the
offensive line. All of us had been letting down on offense,
and our tendency to throw the ball near the goal line
instead of ramming it in didn't help. I didn't feel that it
was just a matter of the linemen failing to block. In any
case, some of the guys were furious. Guard Joe O'Donnell
was especially anxious to tell Peters what he thought of
the article. Peters called me about something after the
story came out, and I told him about the reactions. But
he said that he'd known the guys a long time and hadn't
meant to hurt them. "If they're so mad," he added, "let's
hope they take it out on the Patriots."

One player who had nothing to be ashamed of was my
roommate, Robert James. Our special teams had played
a poor game, getting burned by Jerry Levias's returns, but
on every kick Bob James was the first man downfield. A

few times he got hit just as he neared the ball carrier, but still raced through to make tackles. And he even caught that pass from Maguire on the fake punt. Watching the films of that play, Maguire cracked, "See fellas, you can always count on an old pro."

The coach pointed to the run James made after he caught Paul's pass and added, "You can count on some young pros, too."

I was delighted that Robert was doing so well. From the first day I met him, he had been sweating things out, worrying about just making the squad. His wife was expecting a baby, and he constantly expected to be cut and stranded with no money; so it was great to see that the coach was impressed by him. In fact, I understood that the coaches expected him to develop into a star defensive back.

All week the coaches were after me about my head, saying that I might need some special tests. But I felt fairly good, with just an occasional headache bothering me. It seemed to me that they were making a big deal out of nothing. Finally, after a good practice session on Thursday, I agreed to stop by the hospital. The coaches said that it would only take me a couple of minutes, but when I got there, they said that I would have to wait an hour and then the test would take another hour. I hadn't realized what they had in mind. They wanted to take an EEG and put all those electric things on my head and all that crap. I was annoyed and told them I'd come back the next day. I wasn't going to waste a lot of time hanging around there or worrying about an injury that I was sure meant nothing.

I had another good workout Friday and was really looking forward to the game. We were going to run the ball at last, and I was certain I could get at least 100 yards. After practice I stopped at the hospital again—and underwent a test that I couldn't believe. They put wax on my head and stuck all kinds of damned wires all over me and then put me to sleep. I woke up to find a big nurse—and I mean she was really big—standing over me. She had taken all the wires off me, but she said that she wouldn't let me leave unless I had somebody to drive me home. "Somebody's waiting for me in my car," I lied, anxious to get away.

"What kind of car do you have?"

"A gold Corvette." My Corvette was green. I thought that she'd look for it, fail to find it, and forget about it. But she was too determined for me. She checked with the parking attendant, found out that nobody had come with me, and came back to tell me that I couldn't leave. She was big enough to keep me there, too; looking at her, I thought of the way Houston Antwine had looked on the films. She took me down for some coffee to kill time until the medication wore off. It was two and a half hours before I finally got out of the place.

We stayed at a hotel up in Canada that night instead of having our usual pregame check-in at the Fairfax in downtown Buffalo. A lot of the local kids had learned that we were at the Fairfax, and had made it pretty hard for anyone to get any rest. Since the Boston game was at night and we would have to hang around the hotel all day, it was particularly important that we avoid any disturbances, so the coach chose a hotel near Niagara Falls, about twenty miles from home. "Is the team going to pay for gas and tolls," asked Maguire, "or shall we just deduct it from our taxes?"

Before I left I met with Chuck Barnes, who had flown in with the contracts from Royal Crown Cola. As I signed them, I was amazed once again at how much people believed my name was worth—or at least how much Chuck had convinced them it was worth. Later I had a relaxed dinner at home and—as I tend to do—I misjudged the time. We were due at the hotel at 10:30, and I didn't leave the apartment until 10. I raced up there and arrived five minutes late, but I was happy to see that nobody was checking us that closely. I went into the coffee shop for a milkshake and met a lot of the guys; soon I was having a great time teasing Jack Kemp.

Jack was a real all-American, patriotic type who backed Barry Goldwater and Richard Nixon and was active in Republican politics. He was convinced that the pot-smoking, protesting American youth was dragging our civilization down to hell. I always enjoyed kidding him. "How can you criticize the kids?" I said. "Have you tried grass yourself, Jack?"

"Are you crazy?" he gasped. His face looked as if I'd suggested that he burn down the White House.

"I was at a party tonight," I added, "and a whole lot of hippies were smoking grass, and they all asked me to bring Jack Kemp around to try some."

"They didn't."

"Yeah, they said they'd give you all you want." I hadn't been to any party, of course, but Jack fell for it completely, while all the other guys tried to keep from breaking up.

Later I played cards for a while, then went to my room, where Robert James, as usual, was already asleep. I had never seen a guy who played as hard or slept as much as Bob James. Hoot Gibson, our defensive backfield coach, said that he loved to watch Bob play because he'd never seen anybody go at it so hard. And I guess that was why Bob was always tired. Trying not to wake him, I slipped into my bed, thinking ahead to what I was sure would be one of my best games.

We were just finishing breakfast the next morning when Bill Miller, our offensive end coach, came over and said, "O.J., the coach wants to see you in Room 300." My first thought was that somebody had overheard my jokes about the party the night before, and the coach had been told about it. I was a little worried, but I was pretty sure he'd believe me when I explained that I'd just made up the story to tease Kemp. Unfortunately, that wasn't what he wanted to see me about.

The coach was just sitting in a chair waiting for me as I walked in, and I could see in his face that something was wrong. "I just spoke to the doctor," he said, "and he advised me that you shouldn't play in this game. I'm not going to play you against his orders."

I was really hot. "Then why the hell did he say I was okay yesterday?"

"I guess he hadn't seen all the test results."

"But why did you have to wait until this late to let me know?"

"Take it easy, O.J. This is an important game to us, but your health is more important. Don't let it upset you too much."

He was right, but I couldn't help being angry. There was nothing else to say, so I wheeled around and started out into the hall. Coach Rauch called after me, "I'd like you to suit up for the game anyway."

That was a reasonable enough request, but I was really seething. There is an emotional aspect to getting ready for a football game. The day before, the night before, the warmup—everything goes into getting yourself to an emotional peak. To be shot down right in the middle of that routine was brutal, and now my pent-up emotions needed another outlet. "Hell," I snapped, "I'm not going to suit up for no game unless I'm going to play in it."

Word that I couldn't play spread like wildfire. I talked to some guys who had heard it from total strangers before I had a chance to tell anyone. It's incredible how rumors circulate around football. In fact, the day I went to the hospital and went home without taking the tests, a rumor went out that I had collapsed and died there. Apparently Jack Horrigan had to spend half the night on the phone, telling reporters that the story was false. This time, however, the injury report was sadly accurate: I was out of the game, and it hurt like hell.

I still couldn't understand why I should suit up, and a number of guys, including Maguire, agreed with me. In the afternoon I went home for a while, and by the time I drove over to the stadium with Ben Gregory, the game had actually begun. It was a cold, damp, gloomy night, to match my mood. As I walked to our bench, the guys were all saying that the coach had been looking for me. They said that he was pretty annoyed.

"Let him fine me," I said. "I don't care." Mentally I resolved that when he came over to fine me, I'd say, "Okay, fine me, but I don't want to hear any preaching about it." As it turned out, he got so involved in the game that he never spoke to me, and when he did see me the next day, there was no mention of the incident. That made me feel a little silly for moping around that way, but at the time, I was so disappointed and angry that I couldn't help myself. It was the first time in my life that I just didn't care what the coach might think or do about me.

It was a hell of a game. Buffalo was out-hitting, out-gaining, and out-playing Boston—but on the scoreboard it was the same old story. We couldn't pull away, because every time we got a big chance we blew it, usually by passing. Wayne Patrick proved what I had been sure about all week—we could run on the Patriots. He broke loose for one 72-yard run and totaled 131 yards for the game, quite a performance for a back who had fumbled three times the week before. Max Anderson, substituting for me, chipped in with 46 yards on only ten carries. On defense, Butch Byrd set up two field goals with an interception and a steal of the ball from rookie running back Carl Garrett. With all that going for us, we should have been far ahead. But we weren't; it was a 13-13 tie in the fourth quarter, when Butch made the steal from Garrett and set us up at the Boston sixteen-yard-line.

Then the familiar pattern unfolded. On first down Wingate, running as strongly as he had all night, bulled for six yards. But on second-and-four, instead of punching into the line again, Jack threw a pass. It was incomplete. He tried another pass, and almost had it intercepted. We settled for a field goal, and everybody on the sideline was upset. It was one time when I felt that I could say "Let's run the ball" without sounding like I wanted to run myself. So I did speak up, but I was drowned out by just about every member of our defensive platoon. They were sure we could have run the ball over and angry that they had only a three-point lead to protect. When Boston kicked a field goal to tie it at 16-16, the mood on the bench got even angrier.

Obviously the players weren't the only ones who were mad. On our next series, Coach Rauch sent James Harris in at quarterback. The Patriots immediately started blitzing like crazy, and they did knock us off balance. Then a freak play occurred. James was standing over the center, reading the defense and trying to call an audible, when the whistle blew. An official was calling a delay-of-game penalty. Everybody on the line stood up, but James automatically turned and handed the ball to Max Anderson, who ran on through the hole. The play was dead, but John Bramlett, a linebacker, came up and really nailed

Max. He slammed Max in the face with a vicious forearm, and Max went down on his back with his legs still pumping. His jaw was broken and some teeth knocked out. The guys on our bench were outraged. John Pitts, a close friend of Max's, even shouted at the offensive linemen for failing to block for Max. But it was just one of those things. Some guys heard the whistle and some didn't. It was nobody's fault—except Bramlett's.

Ironically, the play had great impact on the game. To replace Max, the coach sent in Preston Ridlehuber, a back he had picked up for the taxi squad before the season. Ridlehuber had been cut by five different teams in a three-year career, but he was a cocky character who had free advice for everybody in practices, so we all called him Coach Ridlehuber. Rauch had activated him on the morning of the game when he found out that I wouldn't be playing. And by coincidence, he went in just as Rauch was getting ready to call for an option pass, a play I had been working on all week. The idea was to roll to the left, make it look like a sweep to draw the cornerback up, and then hit Haven Moses with a deep pass. It worked perfectly, and Preston Ridlehuber became an instant hero as his touchdown pass won the game, 23-16. It was the second time in his career that Preston had picked a choice moment for his best play. When he had played for Rauch in Oakland in 1968, he had scored one touchdown—but it came in the famous "Heidi" game when he picked up a Jet fumble on a kickoff and ran it in.

I was still pretty sore about missing the game, and critics later pointed out that it had not been one of the classic demonstrations of football; but overall it felt very good to win. The locker room was lively, except for Jack Kemp, who was clearly unhappy about being benched. Old Wayne Patrick just couldn't stop smiling; he had come up with his best game when he needed it most. Afterwards a lot of us went to a party at Booker Edgerson's apartment, and the celebration went on and on. In that weird Eastern Division race, our 2-3 record still kept us in contention. All we needed was one genuine upset to get us rolling—an upset, for example, of the Oakland Raiders.

Chapter Twelve

Homecoming

The Oakland game presented possibilities for a perfect dramatic script. John Rauch was returning to the scene of his greatest coaching triumphs, with a chance to whip his old team as well as his former boss, Al Davis. I was making my first pro appearance in the Bay Area, where I had starred in high school and junior college. And the Bills had an opportunity to turn a stumbling, hesitant start into a successful season with a victory over one of football's strongest teams.

As dreamlike as it may have sounded later, it all seemed possible at the time. The Raiders had won four games and tied another, but they had been having their troubles, barely salvaging games that they had been expected to win easily. With my adrenaline pumped up by the Bay Area crowd and my legs rested from my enforced layoff, I was confident that I could have a good game. And I knew that Rauch would drive us to the limit to beat the Raiders. In a number of ways, I thought that our performance against Oakland might set the tone for our entire season. And in all the wrong ways, I turned out to be correct. We were smothered 50-21, in a stunning rout that sent us skidding

out of contention. We just didn't know how to follow a
ready-made dramatic script for heroes.

On Sunday, with a rare day off after our Saturday night
victory over the Patriots, I called Al Cowlings to hear
about the USC–Stanford game—a game that *did* stick to
a familiar script. When a game is close, there is no way
Stanford can beat USC. I don't know if it's tradition,
coaching, or luck—probably a little of all three—but USC
will always win the close ones from Stanford. In my senior
year we had beaten them, 27-24; this time, Al told me,
USC had won on a field goal at the final gun. Clarence
Davis, who had replaced me at running back, had gained
over 100 yards, and Jimmy Jones, the black sophomore
quarterback, had enjoyed another good game. Even from
3,000 miles away, it was great to listen to Al and share a
little in that winning spirit. Later Tippy and Barbara Day
came over, and we watched the Ram–49er game on television, another game that went according to form. The
49ers against the Rams are like Stanford against USC;
they always manage to lose the close ones. We watched
them blow it in the last quarter, and then went to the
black businessmen's cocktail party that Booker Edgerson
had asked us to attend.

It was a good affair. Most of the team showed up, as
well as Coach Rauch. I hadn't spoken to the coach since
the game, and I was leery about approaching him because
I thought he might still be annoyed at my late arrival. But
he just said, "O.J., we've got a week of hard work ahead
of us. You'll have a lot a bad days, but the mark of the
great ones is that they come right back." That was something I had often said to young kids, and hearing it from
the coach, I felt silly for letting myself get so upset over
my bad luck in missing the Boston game. But at least I
wasn't going to be fined or lectured about it. The party got

livelier as it went on; they had a good band, and everyone was dancing and getting to know one another. I was grateful to Booker for convincing so many of us to be there. We had been too isolated from the Buffalo community, black as well as white, and it was good to get to know some of the local people. Perhaps more important, we were still pretty isolated from one another. Any gathering that brought so many of us together seemed like a worthwhile project.

I checked into the hospital for another EEG the next day. The doctor, sensing that I was still annoyed at him for telling me I could play and then changing his mind, patiently explained everything he was doing to me. He showed me the graph of my brain waves and what he had been looking for, and he assured me that I was fully recovered and ready to go.

Again I was concerned with several off-the-field matters. Marquerite was planning to fly to San Francisco to see her mother, and then to L.A. to look at furniture for our house. RC Cola wanted me to arrange a trip to Las Vegas for a big press conference to announce my contract with the company; Chevrolet wanted me to shoot a commercial on the same day. But I told Bruce Barnes to make any necessary arrangements and just let me know because I was determined not to worry about anything but football that week. By missing a game, I had almost fallen out of contention in the rushing statistics; but Oakland was a team I could get a lot of yardage against. More important, the Raiders were a team we could beat if we ran the ball at them.

It was not a smooth week of preparation. Coach Rauch was understandably tense about facing Al Davis and the Raiders, and his temper flared a number of times during practices. In fact, his relations with most of the young players were becoming very strained. One of the rookies started calling him Satan—because he put you through hell every time you made a mistake—and soon we all picked up the nickname. James Harris complained that all Satan's screaming had messed up his thinking and play-calling during the games; Bill Enyart said that he was mixed up in the same way, and almost all the young players agreed that the coach had been pretty rough on them.

Later, when I began to understand Coach Rauch more fully, I saw how we had misjudged his actions. He was a man with a fierce desire to win, and he was accustomed to men who shared that attitude. When he cursed one of us for blowing an assignment or snapped out a bitter answer to a question, he meant no special offense. He was merely treating us as grown men who should have shared his consuming interest in doing a job perfectly. But many of us had been treated more sympathetically in college, and we were slow to adjust to the pro method. I think that Rauch's disposition made it even harder to take his criticisms. He was such a quiet, gentlemanly coach that his occasional outbursts really shook us. Maybe Vince Lombardi or Norm Van Brocklin would have been easier to face because we would have *expected* them to be very strict and tough. From Rauch, we had no way of expecting trouble—so when it came, we were unable to handle it as well as we should have.

The tension between the coach and me had been building in minor ways for several weeks. I had missed some assignments and fouled up some plays, and he had been right to get mad. I had also done some sloppy blocking, but I thought that he had been unfair in criticizing me for that. Overall my blocking had been good and I felt that, watching from a bad angle on the sideline during the heat of a game, he had been too quick to knock me. Finally, I had flared up over missing the Boston game. All in all, we had no serious problems; there were just a few routine misunderstandings that a more experienced player probably would have shrugged off completely. But I wasn't that experienced, and in the back of my mind, I knew that sooner or later I would have to challenge the coach. I liked and respected him, but I knew that I would have to air my disagreements with him.

Things came to a head on Wednesday—defensive day. As we'd expected, the coach was working the hell out of us for the Raider game; it was our toughest defensive day of the year, and I did more running than I'd ever done in practice. We were really going after the defensive guys and I felt good—but after a while I ran a play the wrong way.

"O.J.," yelled the coach, "you're not supposed to do that. You've got to learn to run your plays right."

I was upset and I came back determined to run the play just right. I thought he had said to run the same play over again. But he had switched the play and I hadn't paid attention, so I wound up doing the exact opposite of what I was supposed to do.

"God damn it, O.J.," he said, "you've got to start learning your plays and concentrating."

"What was the play?" I asked. "I thought we were running the same one over."

"I don't give a damn what you thought. You've just got to learn your plays, you know. It's damn late in the year for you to be blowing your assignments."

I really got mad. On the next play I ran a pass pattern. The ball was thrown to me and I didn't even try to catch it. I couldn't remember doing anything like that since high school; I was acting like a spoiled kid. But I was so mad that I just ignored the ball. As it passed over my shoulder, I casually reached up and slapped it down, and then I turned to see what the coach would do.

"Come on back, let's hustle," he called. I put my head down, ran to the huddle, and turned my back on him. He was pretty hot about it, but he was more adult than I was, so he wasn't about to enter into my childish little argument. I didn't make any more mistakes that day, and I didn't hear any more from him—although the other guys said that he was still steaming about it.

After practice some of the guys started teasing me. "Looks like you're going to get Satan fired," said Charley Ferguson. "Mr. Wilson will break Satan's contract before he breaks yours." The others added, "It's either Satan or O.J. Somebody's got to go"—and a lot of other crap. I told them that they were crazy. It was no big feud, and I was pretty sure it would all be forgotten.

It wasn't my day. When I got home Marquerite told me that I had completely forgotten about a dinner date the night before. A local family had invited us; they had spent half the day preparing a special meal of all the things I liked—and I had gotten into a card game and let the whole night slip by. When I found out about it, I sent them two dozen roses and called to apologize, but I could tell that they were very disappointed in me, and I felt awful.

In our offensive drill Thursday, our fullbacks did most of the running. At first I thought it was a sign that the coach was still mad at me, and I began to worry. But the real reason was that Wayne Patrick had a cold. The coach thought that he might have to use Enyart in the game so he wanted both of them to get plenty of work. The important thing to me was that we were doing a lot of running; our game plan was to run at the Raiders, and no matter who did the running, I was confident that the plan would work.

Kemp did most of the practice quarterbacking. After Jack had been taken out of the Patriot game, some of us had expected Harris to take over. But the coach apparently thought that we'd need Jack's experience against the tricky Raider defense. I was struck by that aspect of Coach Rauch's approach. He had been angry at Jack during the last game and he had been angry at me the day before, but now he was counting heavily on both of us. As a thorough pro, Rauch refused to get emotional or harbor any bad feelings.

I put Marquerite on a plane for the Coast on Thursday. She was happy to get out there for a few days because it was really starting to get cold in Buffalo. I couldn't wait to get there myself; it would be a great homecoming. My legs felt lighter and quicker than they had in weeks, our game plan called for plenty of running, and I had made a resolution that I thought would bring me a big day. I had decided to forget the coaches' instructions for a while and go back to my basic style of running. Most of our sweeps were designed to go far to the outside, and the coaches had told me over and over to stay wide. But too often our blocking just didn't give me time to go wide, and the defensive backs would come up to force me out of bounds with no gain. In the preseason games I had been doing well by making my cuts when I wanted to, the way I had in college. I decided to try it my way once more. If I gained yards, fine; if I screwed up, well, I'd take the full blame for it.

Maguire set up a testimonial dinner for Sestak during the week, and a number of us went to honor Tom. Naturally Maguire was a great toastmaster and the affair was a lot of laughs, but it also made me realize how quickly things changed in pro football. Only a few months earlier I had watched Sestak in camp, fighting to stay with the team. When he had been cut, I had wondered what the Bills' scene would be like without him. But by midseason, he seemed far removed, the part of a distant past. He was busy scouting for the Bills and watching over the bar that he owned with Maguire, and he seemed much older than he had appeared in camp. He was already a character from another era. For better or worse, we were a young team looking ahead to a new era. Listening to Maguire's reminiscences, I hoped that we young players would someday have just as many proud and happy memories as he and Sestak did.

On the plane to San Francisco, I played gin with John Pitts. John wasn't a real gambler. He didn't play cards too often, and when he did, he was shrewd, cautious, and defensive. Since the rest of us were free-wheeling, aggressive card players, John beat us almost every time he played poker or gin. But on that day I beat him badly, adding to my high spirits as I stepped off the plane in my hometown.

My first stop in San Francisco was Galileo High School, where they were having a ceremony to name my old high-school field after me. The crowd started yelling when I walked in, and I looked around and saw many old friends and teammates. Galileo was a small school and had never had much of a football team, but we had enjoyed some stunning upsets. The best came during my senior year when I scored three second-half touchdowns and we broke St. Ignatius's twenty-three-game winning streak. Some high school fans claimed that it had been the biggest upset ever scored in the Bay Area.

Looking at my old school surroundings, however, I remembered a lot more than football games. High school was a time of fighting and hustling, shooting craps and acting cool—and sometimes risking my whole future. The ghetto streets offered many traps for a kid just learning that he can make it in the straight world—and I veered dangerously close to most of them. Once Al Cowlings, a fullback named Joe Bell, and I were caught shooting craps in the school men's room on the day of a junior varsity game we were supposed to play in. The coach found us and marched us into the principal's office; then he turned and stalked out. But when he left, I happened to be standing near the door. The principal began talking only to Al and Joe, and I realized that he thought that I had merely helped the coach bring the other guys in. I saw my chance and I took it; smiling pleasantly, I opened the door and left. The other guys were suspended from school for ten days; I played that same afternoon and scored several touchdowns. Yet the shadow of the affair stayed with me; I was such a wise guy at that time that, if I'd been suspended, I might have quit school and given up football for good. I'll never forget how close I came to disaster, and I'll never stop thanking that principal for failing to notice me by that door.

One lesson, unfortunately, wasn't enough. I was always in and out of scrapes, wondering how long I'd last in school—and in football. Luckily, there always happened to be some dedicated and patient people around to talk me out of my stupid ideas. Scanning the young faces at Galileo last fall, I looked forward to giving the same kind of guidance to a lot of them.

They held a brief ceremony for me at half time, retiring my high school jersey and giving me a big ovation. Then the game continued. Galileo was behind, 20-18, when I arrived, and everybody was sure that I would inspire them to victory. They lost, 44-18, an early indication of what kind of weekend lay ahead.

I stopped by to visit my family and Marquerite's and then drove down to Hayward where the club was staying. Hayward is a dull East Bay town about 20 miles south of Oakland; a lot of us were annoyed that the coach had put us there. Apparently he was afraid that we would get into too much action if we stayed closer to San Francisco. We understood how nervous he was about facing the Raiders, but we still resented being treated so much like little kids. In fact, Coach Rauch was beginning to seem more distant than ever from us.

As I parked at the motel, the coach happened to be walking by. We walked in together; as he spoke, I could feel how tense he was about playing the Raiders. "We can beat them," he said. "We can do it, if we just go after them." At a moment like that, when the coach let himself reveal his true emotions, I felt very close to him. He was a good man, working under tremendous pressure. I realized how much he was counting on me, and I wished that he would take more opportunities to speak personally to us. I wanted to know him better.

That night I had a long argument with Robert James. Nobody on the Bills was changing as dramatically as Bob. When I had first known him, I had teased him about being "country" and "conditioned" by his southern background, and he had just smiled sheepishly and taken it. But a few months around some of the sophisticated blacks on our club had given him a new self-confidence. In Oakland he finally exploded at me: "Just what do you mean by 'country,' O.J.? I'm getting awful tired of all that crap." I tried to explain what I had meant, but didn't do a very good job—and he wouldn't let me off the hook. I finally gave up and promised not to call him "country" any more, but he still wanted to argue. It was the first night I'd ever roomed with him when he didn't just want to go to sleep. He was determined to stand up to me, no matter how long it took. That night I got to know the new Robert James.

I took Bill Enyart into San Francisco on Saturday; he

was anxious to change his image, too, by buying a lot of new clothes. He had been needled all season about his white wool socks and conservative tweed jackets, and he insisted that I show him a store with some mod threads. He picked out some pin-striped, double-breasted suits and jackets and broke out in that goofy grin of his as he tried them on. "Oh, Bill, you're getting ready," I said. "You're really getting ready." As usual, he laughed at himself and said, "Aw, O.J." But he didn't back down. He bought a lot of wild stuff and went back to tell everybody about his new image.

Dinner was a strange scene. All the guys were talking about going to shows and things, trying to see some of the area while they had a chance. As nervous as the coach was, I was worried that he would hear all the talk and get annoyed that we were thinking of anything but the next day's game. Then Booker Edgerson came in, laughing and yelling at a lot of the guys. It was obvious that he had been having a few drinks, and we all tried to shoo him down and keep him out of trouble. After the meal everybody drifted off, and I was surprised to find that I had nobody to take into San Francisco with me. Finally I found Willie Grate, another "country" guy on the team, who had never seen California before.

Riding across the Bay Bridge, he asked me where Alcatraz was, and I pointed it out. Then he said, "Is it true that they have alligators in the water around it?" I broke up—imagine alligators in the San Francisco Bay? Later I told a few guys that Willie had been looking for alligators, and they teased him quite a bit. He got mad at me again and I felt bad about it, but I couldn't help laughing every time I thought of those 'gators. We stopped at a few places in San Francisco, drove back to Hayward, and got a good night's sleep. I woke up Sunday feeling great. It was a beautiful sunny day, about 70 degrees; they expected a record crowd—and I was ready to go out and show something to the Oakland fans.

The game was just ridiculous. We made every mistake you can make in a football game. We fumbled, we were intercepted, we missed assignments; we did all the things you can't afford to do against an explosive team like the Raiders or a quarterback like Daryle Lamonica. On the first play of the game, Butch Byrd had a sure interception in his hands and dropped it—and we might as well have gone home. A few plays later Billy Cannon juggled a short pass over the middle, finally grabbed it, and scored a 53-yard touchdown. We gave them the ball back on three fumbles, an interception, and one of Maguire's rare poor punts—and Lamonica took advantage of every break. As incredible as it seemed, he threw six touchdown passes in the first twenty-eight minutes of the game. We were shellshocked: They had a 42-0 lead.

I started out as if it would be my best game. On our first few series of plays, I carried six times for 50 yards —better than 8 yards a carry. I felt loose, confident, ready to roll. But I never touched the ball again. As the score mounted, we passed more and more, and when we did run, Bill Enyart was the ball carrier. When Kemp couldn't move us at all, Jim Harris came in and threw a touchdown pass to Haven Moses; it looked as if he might finally win the starting job. He led the team fairly well, completed eight of sixteen passes, and appeared to be our only bright spot in the gruesome afternoon. But in the fourth quarter Jim's knee, which had sidelined him in college, crumpled under him again. He was lost for the season.

As the game dragged on, I began to get angrier. We were obviously out of it and I knew we couldn't settle down and run the ball. But I was accustomed to being used by my team even if we were behind. I expected to at least have some passes thrown toward me, but I never did. I just ran one swing pattern after another, strictly as a decoy. It felt as if I ran a hundred swing patterns—and it was by far the longest afternoon of my career. It wasn't any easier for Coach Rauch. He paced the sidelines, bursting with anger and frustration, but there was nothing he could do to stop the embarrassment.

Marlin Briscoe replaced Bubba Thornton at flanker in the second half and, as always, made several spectacular plays. Everybody on the team had thought for a couple of weeks that Marlin should have been starting. Bubba had great speed, but Marlin had a much better knack for breaking into the clear and he came up with big catches. Marlin said that he had a clause in his contract that guaranteed him more money if he started a certain number of games, so he didn't expect to start. But at Oakland, he made it virtually impossible for anyone to keep him on the bench with six catches for over 100 yards. I was certain that he would be the starter from then on. As a matter of fact, I figured that we would see other changes; the coach wasn't going to take a 50-21 loss to Oakland very calmly. Unfortunately, however, the one change that could have made the biggest difference was out of the question. They operated on Jim Harris's knee the next day.

Chapter Thirteen

The Low Point

An athlete lives by hope and confidence. I've never gone into a football game, a 100-yard dash, or anything else without thinking that I could win. Yet during the long midseason weeks, as we slipped from a 2-3 record to a 2-7 mark, I couldn't help tempering my optimism with a harder view of reality. Incredibly, the second-place Houston Oilers were stumbling so badly that we retained a mathematical chance for the playoffs until the last week of the season; so in one sense, it was easy to keep saying that we could recover from each disaster and sneak into the playoffs. But the fact was that we *weren't* recovering, and I began to feel a little silly about telling myself each week, "This is the game. This time I'll have a big day and we'll get going." The weeks were passing and the Bills were going nowhere, and idle dreaming would not be enough to turn things around.

We needed many things, from simple blocking, tackling, and executing, to more elusive factors, like togetherness and confidence. Each fumble, each touchdown pass by Lamonica, and each humiliating newspaper story about the Raider game showed how much we lacked. But the crucial problem could be summed up in a sentence: halfway through the season, we still weren't a team.

The Oakland game illustrated that fact graphically and brutally. The defense seemed to let the horrible mistakes of the offense get it down. The offensive players, watching a dependable man like Booker Edgerson suffer through one of the worst games of his life, seemed to lose even more hope. The easy thing to do would have been to blame Rauch or Kemp, Booker or Butch—or any of the other guys who had bad games. But that was our trouble; we spent too much time looking for easy ways out of our crises. We had to face the fact that the real solution would be much harder. I knew that it was time for me to stop kindling my own hopes each week, and turn my full attention to the more basic challenge of helping the Bills to become a genuine team.

Strangely, the Oakland slaughter didn't seem to be the jolt we needed. I had expected to report to practice and find a group of bitter, aggressive athletes determined to go to any lengths to prove themselves and regain their pride. Yet the mood was remarkably casual. I realized that the professional approach was to take defeats in stride, but for once I wondered if maybe we should stop being so professional and act a little more like rookies. We had lost to what was probably the greatest team in football, and maybe some people thought that we should accept that calmly. But we had also lost 50-21, in a pitiful excuse for a contest. There was no way I thought we should accept *that* so calmly. I wondered what kind of jolt it would take to force us to really get mad and apply ourselves to the job. Then I found out. We lost to the Miami Dolphins.

The Dolphins were 0-5-1 before they played us, but they were probably the best team that ever managed to go six games without a victory. Watching their defense on the films, I thought that Nick Buoniconti was as quick a middle linebacker as I'd ever seen. They also had a very solid defensive line led by rookie Bill Stanfill. It was a good defense and a hustling defense, and it looked as if it would be tough to run against. The coaches apparently got the same impression because our game plan called for a lot of passing. This didn't exactly boost my spirits because even when our plan called for running, we'd pass; I shuddered to think of how often we'd pass in Miami.

Marquerite had stayed in Los Angeles for the week, so I spent a few evenings out with Ben Gregory and some other guys. Both during and after practices, most of the club seemed to have a fairly lighthearted attitude. As disappointed as the coach had been, he seemed to shake off the Oakland loss and get right down to business again; so I figured that I might as well get that Raider game out of my own mind. Coach Rauch was still getting on me quite a bit in practices, and some of the guys were still kidding about how I was going to get him fired. They were calling me the big superstar, and when Ben hung around me, they called him Bud Jones.

The Bud Jones thing was a constant joke on our team. Bud Jones was the shuffling Negro porter in the commercials advertising the TWA million-dollar bonus for employees. In the commercials, he would help a customer who was limping to the counter, grinning and saying, "I'm Bud Jones, sir, J-O-N-E-S," to try to get his piece of that bonus money. So whenever a brother would go out of his way to do something and grin, the other brothers would say, "That a way, Bud Jones." It was just a joke; it didn't mean that a guy was really Uncle Tomming, just that he was grinning or being too servile for a minute. Willie Grate, for example, had a habit of smiling everytime a coach said something to him, so we always needled him about Bud Jonesing. And then the guys started claiming that Ben was Bud Jonesing around me.

Bill Enyart also came in for a share of kidding because of an article in one of the Buffalo papers. Bill had enjoyed a good second half in Oakland, making a total of 68 yards in ten carries, and he was quoted as saying that the game had given him the confidence he needed. He also referred to his friendly battle with Wayne Patrick for the fullback job, and at the end he added, "It's too bad we don't have a fight like that for every position."

"Ah," said Maguire, "it's about time. We were due for the good old dissension-on-the-team story." All the older guys rode Bill pretty hard about it, saying, "Glad you've got that confidence, Bill. Wish we were all fighting for our positions with that old confidence." Bill took it in his standard way, just smiling and saying in his backwoods drawl, "Aw, fellas, come on."

I went to the hospital every day to see James Harris. He went through a lot of pain with his knee, but the worst pain had to be in his mind. All season he had seemed to be on the edge of something big. In the Jets game he was missing his passes by inches, against Denver he had gotten confused, and then against Boston and Oakland he had begun to look like a real quarterback. I imagined what must have gone through his mind, coming off the bench with us trailing 35-0, and those rugged Raider linemen just teeing off on us. But he had kept his poise and impressed all of us, and there could be no doubt that he would have been our quarterback for the rest of the season. He had overcome the pressures of being a black quarterback, a rookie, and a newcomer to a complicated system—and then his damn knee had taken the reward away from him. He couldn't help but be way down as he lay in that bed, and he was a little bitter because Coach Rauch hadn't called or come to see him. He never did hear from the coach while he was in the hospital. We assumed that the coach was so wrapped up in his job and the future that he didn't even give a thought to a past injury or to an emotional approach to an injured player. But for Jim, who had been used to the fatherly way Eddie Robinson treats his Grambling players, it was a little hard to understand.

Jim was pretty worried for a while because he hadn't really studied the fine print in his contract and wasn't sure if he'd get paid for the rest of the season. When he learned that he would get his money, he felt a little better, and we had some pleasant sessions in his room. He always seemed to have three or four girls visiting him, and at least a half-dozen ballplayers stopped by each day. We all did a lot of kidding around, and for a hospital room, it became a fairly lively place. I was more certain than ever that if James could ever shake off his bad luck with injuries, he would command the respect of the team and become a hell of a leader.

Buffalo was getting awfully cold and even a little snowy, so it felt good to land in Miami. As apprehensive as I was about Buoniconti and the rest of that Miami defense, I felt anxious to get a shot at them. The day before the game, I got a chance to talk to Mercury Morris, the rookie runner from West Texas State. I told him I envied him for playing in that weather, but he said that I shouldn't envy a black player in Miami—the social life left a lot to be desired. It was something to think about. Buffalo wasn't one of the swinging capitals of the Western World, but at least blacks were treated with some respect. A losing season would have seemed even longer if you had to live with racial slurs. Strange as it may have been, I felt a tinge of gratitude toward frigid Buffalo. And I knew that the city would seem a lot warmer if we went back to it with a victory.

We didn't just lose the damn game. We handed it to Miami on a silver platter. As bad as I'd felt in Oakland, I felt worse during the Miami game. The Dolphins had promoted the game as "Victory Sunday," and the mayor had even made a special proclamation. As Jim Peters wrote the next morning in the *Buffalo Courier-Express,* "The mayor must have done a good job of scouting suitable opponents to select this day." We weren't laughing, of course, but you couldn't blame the press or the public for laughing at us in that game. We played with all the finesse of a slapstick comedy team.

It had to be my personal low point. I gained a total of 12 yards in ten carries. I had nightmares about Buoniconti for days afterward. Early in the game I nailed him with a very good block, and he made me pay for it all day. Everywhere I went, he seemed to be waiting for me. I knew all about Butkus and Nobis and the others who were supposed to be so great, but on that afternoon, I would have preferred to face any of them rather than Buoniconti.

As terrible as my game was, it wasn't quite as bad as the statistics indicated. It seemed as if I was always carrying the ball on third down with short yardage to go, with the defense really stacked against me. And I made some good moves in the open field with swing passes. I caught four for 32 yards and had two longer ones called back by penalties, and I honestly felt that I was faking their outside linebackers pretty well. But their middle linebacker was a different story. Buoniconti not only stopped me again and again, but he came up with a big interception in Miami territory to stop one of our many threats.

I still wince when I think about that game. George

Saimes intercepted Bob Griese's first pass and returned it to the Miami twenty-seven. We settled for a field goal. Mercury Morris fumbled the next kickoff and Pete Richardson recovered for us on their twenty-five—but Kemp got intercepted by Buoniconti. That was the pattern of the game: Five times we had the ball inside the Miami fifteen-yard-line, and we managed a total of two field goals—6 lousy points. The Dolphins made plenty of errors of their own, but eventually rolled over us, 24-6.

Kemp completed fourteen of nineteen passes in the first half, but his key misses near the goal line evidently annoyed Rauch. With the score 14-3 at half time, the coach decided to make a change. I was sitting in front of my locker, staring at the floor, when Dan Darragh came over and said, "Help me, O.J."

I took a moment to realize what he meant. When it sunk in, I was glad. Jack Kemp was a great guy and I really enjoyed talking and arguing with him about football and politics and everything else, but at that point I thought that we desperately needed a change. Darragh, who had only been activated that week, was still unfamiliar with the system; I knew that he couldn't throw as well as Kemp. But we didn't need throwing—we had tried plenty of passing without winning—as much as we needed leadership. I hoped that Darragh could mix up his plays and give us some confidence in our attack. As we headed out onto the field I said, "Come on, Darragh. You can get us going."

He didn't get us going, completing only six of seventeen passes. But I still felt that the team was working a little harder with him in there. I hoped that he would be our starter from then on. When one thing isn't working, I figured, we might as well try something else. One thing was certain: We couldn't get any worse.

Everybody was raging in the locker room, ripping off

their uniforms and cursing at themselves. They kept the door closed to the press and the room became very quiet. First Coach Rauch walked into the center and took the blame himself. He said maybe it was his fault that we had been so disappointing. Then Harry Jacobs stood up and said, "Let's have a meeting Tuesday morning."

I shook my head and said to Haven Moses, "We can have a million damn meetings. That's not going to do a God damn thing. They might have had meetings all last year, too, and it didn't stop them from losing."

Haven agreed, and a few guys sitting near me also nodded. "Meetings won't solve our problem," I added. "The only way we're going to win is to work at it. We blew this damn game."

Chapter Fourteen

The Stormiest Week

While the rest of the team flew back from Miami to Buffalo, I had to detour to Detroit to film a commercial for Chevrolet. I arrived back in Buffalo late Monday night to find that Marquerite and Arnelle had already flown in from the Coast. Marquerite had left the luggage at the airport, so I got up early Tuesday, rushed out to pick it up, and then headed for practice. I noticed that the gas in my Corvette was a little low, but I was running late and I figured I had enough to make it. The way things had been going, I should have known better than to count on my luck. The gas ran out about halfway to practice —and within a block of a gas station. I got out and pushed the car into the station and told the guy to hurry, but I knew I would barely make it in time for practice.

I hustled into the locker room at exactly nine-thirty, the time our regular meetings usually start. I was shocked to see that everybody was already there, and Harry Jacobs was in the middle of the floor, apparently at the climax of a long speech. Suddenly it hit me: I had blown the damn team meeting. When Harry had mentioned it in the locker room at Miami, I had assumed that the reaction was so unfavorable that the idea would be dropped: in fact, I had never given it another thought. But the guys had obviously agreed on the meeting on the plane ride from Miami to Buffalo, and there was no way anyone could have let me know about it in Detroit. Ironically, I would have been on time anyway if I hadn't run out of gas, but that didn't help matters. I was late and everybody knew it.

Harry was in the middle of one of his typical speeches —long, well-organized, and yet emotional. As often as the older guys kidded him about his preaching, Harry never changed his style. Somebody had told me that at one banquet he was asked to introduce Kemp, who was receiving an award, and his introduction went on so long that it sounded like a eulogy and the audience began to wonder if Kemp had died. Maguire said that it was lucky Harry was married and settled down because if he ever tried chasing girls he would convert more of them than he would make.

Harry only had a few minutes to go in his speech when I sat down. He reached his conclusion and then snapped, "Also, I want to thank O.J. for caring enough about his team to show up at the meeting on time."

"You're welcome, Harry," I said. It really made me mad. He had no idea why I might have been late—for that matter, Bob Tatarek had come in only a few minutes before me—and yet Harry decided to single me out and ridicule me as a bad team man. When he asked for questions and suggestions from the floor, I had to bite my tongue to keep from telling him off.

Marlin Briscoe offered one good suggestion: "Our problem is that we don't know each other. Take a guy like Willie Grate. He's been with us for two months and how many of you know where he lives or anything about him? Take a lot of other guys—the same thing applies. The older guys are in their own bag. The younger guys play cards together, but they're not all that close. As a team, we have very little communication."

Both the young and old groups agreed that Marlin had a good point. "At Denver," he went on, "we had a sort of get-together about once a week—just a bull sesion to talk about anything, not especially football. Maybe it would be good if we just had a few drinks and talked and spent more time together." Everyone seemed enthusiastic about the idea of having some parties beyond the ones that Coach Rauch had after our home games. And we agreed that we would start that trend at the coming week's annual Halloween costume party at Ron McDole's.

It was a good, open discussion, and I had the feeling that the Miami defeat might have finally forced us to jell; but I still hadn't cooled off about Harry's snide comment. As we all milled around, waiting for the coaches to reenter the room and start the regular offensive and defensive meetings, I stalked around looking for Harry. I was ready to tell him that I didn't give a damn what he thought. He didn't know a thing about why I was late and he could screw off before I'd tell him why. I was going to tell him that maybe we would have won a few more games if he'd covered his damn man instead of worrying about preaching to everybody. Finally I saw him across the room and started toward him, but Maguire came up to me first.

"Harry shouldn't have done what he did," Paul said.

"Damn right he shouldn't have," I snapped.

"You know," he said, "he had just gone on for half an hour about why we were screwed up because guys were pointing the finger at each other and judging other guys instead of just doing their jobs. And then at the climax of his speech, he turned around and pointed the finger at you. He has a great sense of logic."

It *was* ironic, and the way Maguire told it made me smile. Then I saw Harry coming over to me, with that serious look he gets whenever he's ready to say something important. "I'm sorry," he said, "I shouldn't have said what I did. I was emotionally upset." I forgot all about the angry lecture I had planned to give him. Maguire's comment had made me take the whole thing a little less personally, and the sincere look on Harry's face got to me. Even though I was bitter about his remarks, I couldn't help being impressed that a thirty-two-year-old team captain could be a big enough man to apologize to a rookie. From that point on, I began to understand and appreciate Harry a great deal more.

I recalled an afternoon early in the season when he had approached me after practice and said, "O.J., you can help the team if you talk a little more." I had wondered if he had meant it sarcastically or as a joke; it sounded weird for a recognized team leader to be saying that to a newcomer. But he had repeated the thought again a few weeks later: "Maybe if you yell and get going, O.J., the rest of the guys will, too." I had just passed it off, but after that meeting I realized that he had been trying to use some psychology on me. Instead of saying, "I'm the leader here and you've got to do better," he had been asking me to help him lead. It had been a good, fair approach and thinking about it, I was convinced that no matter how wound-up or overemotional Harry tended to get, he was acting out of an overriding concern for the rest of us.

The team meeting set the stage for the stormiest and most intensely emotional week I've ever experienced in football. In retrospect, it was the week that forged us into at least the beginnings of a real team—and the week that gave us all a reason to hope that, despite all our mistakes before and after it, we had a bright future. Words such as "love" and "pride" are so overused that they become mere clichés in football: Winning teams always claim to have love and pride and losing teams are supposed to be lacking in both. But in the wake of our embarrassingly bad performance in Miami, we slowly began to build a mutual respect that—in some future championship year—I think we may look back upon as a start toward a real love among teammates. And while all athletes must have pride in themselves, it was only in the weeks following that Miami disaster that I developed pride in being a member of the Buffalo Bills.

The new feeling didn't spring up immediately in any of us, and it wasn't produced by any single meeting or speech or player. It was born out of anger and hard work and pain, and I don't think I grasped its whole meaning until I looked back on the season from the calm and distant perspective of California. But it began in midseason, as a 2-5 football team prepared for its first meeting of the season with the Kansas City Chiefs, the team that would go on to become world champions.

The Tuesday workout began with Dan Darragh at quarterback, and his presence gave us a lift. We started out fairly well in a skeleton drill, in which the backs and receivers run patterns and we go up and down the field passing the ball. After a few patterns, we were walking back to the huddle and Briscoe yelled, "Come on, let's really pep it up. Let's run back to those huddles."

Everything picked up speed from that point on. Marlin had always been a potential leader on the team; he was a firm, articulate speaker with a personality that made people respect his words. But he had failed to stick with Denver as a quarterback, mainly because he was just too small at 5′ 10″, and he had left the Broncos with some bitterness. Rauch picked him up on the stipulation that he would be a wide receiver, and he was a little subdued for a while about his inability to become the first black quarterbacking star. In fact, he never gave up his hope of eventually becoming a quarterback. But the fact that Rauch gave Harris such a good shot at the job ruled out any feelings about possible prejudice, so Marlin more or less accepted his new role. And as he made more and more brilliant catches and finally fought his way onto the first team, he also began to speak out more among the guys. His words on the field drove us through one of our snappiest Tuesday practices. When we started running plays as an entire team, we put real sting into them, even though we weren't even wearing pads. If we had been as lively in Miami, we probably would have won the damn game.

The papers poured it on us that week. One writer blasted me for missing holes and screwing up my plays. Another said that our offensive line was opening holes that a respectable moth wouldn't claim. One guy cracked that Al Bemiller had promised the voters that he would retire if he won the election in Cheektowaga; he added that he hoped Al would win and that if Coach Rauch was smart, he would convince the whole line to run for office. Most of us got pretty mad, but for once the anger didn't take the form of bitching. We took it out on the practice field.

The Wednesday workout wasn't a practice; it was a street brawl. Some of the action was good aggressive hitting, but a lot of it was chickenshit. Some of the stuff that went on was just unbelievable, and I refused to agree that it was all just healthy enthusiasm. It was crap, and I said so.

It was defensive day, which meant that we were running Kansas City plays so the defense could get ready for them. In a drill such as that one, you don't go full speed all the time. You run each play at a certain speed and once the defensive men react and move up to hit you, you slow down and they grab you. There isn't any hard tackling—or there isn't supposed to be. The trouble started when I ran a play through a hole off-tackle. Tatarek, who had never been one of my greatest fans anyway, saw me coming and caught me with a quick elbow to the chin. I wasn't looking for the blow and was off balance, so it sent me backwards very quickly. As I was falling, Mike McBath came up and knocked me down.

"Pick yourself up, O.J.," somebody called, and a lot of guys started laughing. I laughed, too, but I was furious. I didn't mind getting knocked down, but there's no reason to get elbowed in the face during a workout. Back in the huddle, somebody said that McBath had been a wise guy; but I wasn't mad at McBath. He had hit me with a shoulder, the way you should hit in a drill like that. As we lined up for the next play, I noticed that my lip was bleeding. I spit a little blood onto the grass. "Tatarek," I thought, "I owe you one."

I never did get him back. In fact, I all but forgot about him because so much else was going on. Things really got out of hand after the defensive drill when the offense began running some plays. On those plays the routine is similar to the defensive one: You run your play through the hole and about 5 yards past the line, and if a defensive back is there, he slaps or grabs you. But after a few plays, Wayne Patrick went through a hole and Pete Richardson, playing strong safety, came up and nailed him. It was incredible. There was no way in the world that Pete could have flattened Wingate the way he did if Wingate had been running full speed. But Wingate had been slowing up, and for some reason Pete slammed him down.

The defensive guys started laughing and yelling, "That's the way to hit." Wingate came back to the huddle and said, "When I get a shot at him, I'm going to nail his ass."

It was weird. We had run that drill all year without any contact, and now Pete not only hit him, but got encouragement from the rest of the defense.

A minute later I ran through a hole and slowed down to a jog—and out of nowhere came my God damn roommate Robert James. I was slowing up, not even looking toward him, and he came at me full speed and nailed me. As I got up, I slammed the ball down and stared at him, but he was already trotting away, looking very pleased with himself. And then I realized that in addition to the defensive guys, even the coaches were yelling, "Yeah, that's the way to hit. Knock him on his ass." I didn't know what the hell they were thinking about. I guessed that they were happy to see a lot of enthusiasm on the field. But there was still no reason to cheer that chickenshit kind of hitting. We would run six or seven plays as usual and then on the eighth one, when we were least expecting it, one of those clowns would sneak up and nail us. To me, that was nothing to cheer about. But Ralph Hawkins, the linebacker coach, was clapping and yelling, "Keep up that good hitting."

Bob James nailed Bill Enyart, too, before the drill ended —just to make sure that nobody escaped. The defense got another good laugh out of that, but we were really seething. As we finally came off the field, I said to Maguire, "I don't care what the coaches or anybody else say, that was chickenshit football." I spoke as loudly as I could, hoping that Coach Hawkins would hear me. "Everybody thinks it's very funny, but meanwhile Wingate and Bill and I are getting the shit knocked out of us without even expecting it. It's one thing to hit during a full scrimmage when our linemen are blocking and we're going full speed, but it's another to hit a guy who isn't even watching for you."

Bill Enyart had some words with Pete Richardson in

the locker room. "If Coach Hawkins thinks that sneak hitting is so good," Bill added, "why doesn't he get out there and let me run at him?" Then Wingate went up to Robert James and said, "I'll see that you get yours tomorrow."

"Well," said Robert, "we were just trying to keep you guys awake." The words sounded strange coming from him. When he had joined us, he wouldn't have talked like that to anyone. If he had said anything, he would have been nice and polite about it. He probably would have apologized. But the new Robert wasn't going to be called country anymore by me or anyone else. He wore pin-striped double-breasted suits and he said, "Nothin' to it, baby" when you asked him something. Some of us kidded him when he began to change, saying, "Oh, look at Robert, he's wearing his boots." But Robert wasn't even going to take that for long. He was getting as tough off the field as he was on it.

I went to bed early Wednesday night and got almost twelve hours of sleep. I was glad I did because Thursday's workout was even more heated. It was offensive day, so we had the initiative. At the first opportunity, Enyart ran into Pete Richardson so hard that he almost killed him. Bill, who was about 6' 4" and 240 pounds, didn't really have to run into Pete, who weighed about 200, but he went out of his way to make his point. Patrick and I didn't feel too bad about it, either. Then Bob Kruse, an offensive guard, got into a fistfight with Dave Ogas, a middle linebacker. Both men had been picked up after being cut by Oakland, but it didn't look as if they had ever had time to make friends.

The biggest battle, however, was between defensive lineman Julian Nunamaker and offensive guard Joe O'Donnell. Joe wasn't the kind of player you would ever expect to see fighting. He was a quiet, workmanlike guard from

Michigan who was in his fifth year with the Bills. Looking at him—he was pretty bald—and talking to him, I always considered him a real old pro. He didn't appreciate it when I told him how old I thought he was, but other than that, we had become good friends. Joe was a very steady type who never got excited. But for two straight plays he and Nunamaker busted one another unusually hard—and on the third play a fight broke out. They really swung into it; I couldn't see what O'Donnell hit him with, but whatever it was, it was potent. Joe stepped back and Nunamaker was writhing on the ground, groaning. He lay there for several minutes, and by the time he got up, everybody was laughing at him. I wondered if that would make him even angrier, but when he looked around, Julian started laughing along with us. On our team, if you take your lumps you might as well laugh because everybody's going to laugh at you anyway. Julian seemed to sense that, and the affair blew over quickly. But the mood of the club remained tense and belligerent. A lot of raw emotion had been exposed on a team that had glided through seven games without too much communication. I wasn't sure how that emotion and anger would be expressed when we took the field against the Chiefs.

Events calmed down on Friday, as we had a light drill and posed for some publicity pictures. The picture session gave Maguire a chance to get everybody into a relaxed mood again. For a while he kept insisting that we rotate blacks and whites; he called the blacks Oreos and the white guys Lorna Doones. He also told J.C. Collins that he ought to come to McDole's costume party hugging his white wife—they would be an Oreo cookie. It was another example of the kind of remark that only Maguire could get away with. We had a very black-conscious team; a word like "nigger" would never be tolerated, and racial jokes would have caused a lot of trouble if they had come from anyone but Maguire. Yet Paul's sense of humor was so sharp and his timing so perfect that he could get away with comments that would have started fights if anyone else had made them. As a matter of fact, the blacks on the team considered him one of the most popular players.

Our outlook on the season was subtly changing. We were still in contention for second place, if only because the Oilers appeared likely to stumble. But we were no longer thinking in terms of magically turning things around. We faced back-to-back games against Kansas City and the Jets, so we began to think of ourselves as spoilers, with a chance to mess up the plans of some of the leaders while we got our own club going. Early in the year I had made a habit of looking at the schedule and guessing which games we could win and Houston could lose. The Miami game had cured me of that; it was one game I had been confident that we could win, and the defeat had made my guessing seem more like dreaming. Kansas City had a great team, and we couldn't afford the luxury of rooting against Houston or looking ahead to easier games on our schedule. We needed every bit of concentration just to cope with the Chiefs. And we had the special challenge of channeling all the anger that had been building during the week into a concerted effort on the field.

On a cold, gray, drizzly Buffalo Sunday, slugging it out on a muddy field against the strongest physical team in the league, we had very little to be ashamed about. Our defense was superb, holding the Chiefs without a touchdown until the final two minutes of the game. With Dan Darragh at quarterback, our offense moved crisply at times, but once again, we couldn't quite make the important plays. Darragh called a cool game, mixing runs and passes and guiding us to several decent drives. He gave the ball to me sixteen times and to Wingate twelve times, and we managed 107 yards between us against the best rushing defense in the league. But unfortunately, Dan still wasn't throwing the ball too well. After only a few weeks of work, his timing was off and his arm fairly weak. Even when he completed some passes early, his throws wobbled. And when those mighty Chief pass rushers started teeing off on him later in the day, he seemed to be a little slow getting rid of the ball; they nailed him nine times for a total of 93 yards, often throwing us for key losses after we had worked our way into field goal range.

Meanwhile Jan Stenerud, whose field goal range is 50 yards, was keeping Kansas City in the game. We scored first, on a refreshing new development: Given the ball on a fumble on the Chief seventeen-yard-line, we actually converted it into a touchdown. Stenerud made it 7-3 at the half and 7-6 after three periods, but we seemed to be hanging on. In fact, we came off the field a few times in the first half without scoring—and actually heard the fans cheering us. The astute Buffalo fans seemed to appreciate the fact that we were moving the ball at all, and I was sure that they liked the idea of us running for some big first downs instead of going pass-crazy. Even though he wasn't getting us points, Darragh helped the defensive unit in one way; because we were running, we were giving the defenders quite a bit more rest on the sidelines. At the beginning of the second half, for example, we controlled the ball for eight minutes. Dan showed us a lot of leadership—more than the score might have indicated.

The final score was Kansas City 29, Buffalo 7, but it was misleading as hell. They had to bring Lenny Dawson off the bench at the half to replace quarterback Mike Livingston, who couldn't do anything right against our defense. And even when Stenerud chipped away with three fourth-period field goals to give them a 15-7 lead, we still came within inches of a touchdown that, with a 2-point conversion, might have salvaged a tie for us. I ran a pattern over the middle and was wide open, but the pass was just a little too high. I was sure I could go all the way for the touchdown if I could pull it down, and I leaped high enough to get a fingertip on it—just enough to deflect it up and into the waiting arms of Chief safety Johnny Robinson. He returned the interception into our territory, and our defense, after fifty-eight gallant minutes, finally began to crack.

Mike Garrett broke loose for a 34-yard touchdown run to clinch the game, and another interception put them deep in our territory again as the clock ran out. But Kansas City coach Hank Stram didn't let it run out. He called time with three seconds to go, sent in a play, and watched Garrett scoot 5 yards around end for a final touchdown that was an ironically fitting conclusion to our angry week. The fans booed for several minutes after the game; I later learned that on some parlay-betting cards in Buffalo, the Chiefs had been 17-point favorites, so the last touchdown had been expensive for some Buffalo bettors. It also annoyed Coach Rauch, who said, "I beat Stram, forty-one to six, with Oakland last year in the division playoff, but I don't recall calling any timeout as the clock ran out." And the defensive players, who took the last score as a personal insult from Stram, were raging as we left the field. Harry Jacobs even raced over to the Chiefs' bench to tell Stram off.

Personally, I wasn't all that upset about it. I believe that football is a sixty-minute game and you have the right to use every bit of time that's available to you. I thought Stram could have been more sportsmanlike by letting the clock run out, but I also figured that he had every right to use the final seconds if he wanted to. I assumed that he might have wanted his team to try a certain play from the five-yard-line, and he might have been trying to avoid any careless habits—the kind that so often kept us from scoring. And finally, I didn't really give much of a damn whether we had lost 22-7 or 29-7. We knew that we had done some things very well, regardless of what the score showed. In any case, Stram went on to win the Super Bowl; how much can anybody fault his methods?

The defensive men, of course, took it very differently. Hours after the game, at our weekly get-together at the Fairfax, some of them were still cursing about Stram. I realized that I had missed the point of their anger. They had fought one of the most courageous battles of the season to hold the explosive Chiefs without a touchdown for almost an entire game. They had even suffered two casualties in the fight. George Saimes, our tough, smart free safety, had a damaged knee that would finish him for the season. Paul Guidry, our left linebacker, had a separated shoulder. Guidry had been one of the lesser-known stars of our defense; fast and strong, he had been playing well enough to earn All-Pro selection if the team had been winning more games. And his dedication was typical of the entire defense that day. He had separated his shoulder in the first period and reinjured it in the third, yet he finished the game. After putting up that kind of effort, the defenders saw the final touchdown as a brutal and unnecessary jab.

After the game I had a chance to talk with Mike Garrett, who had won the Heisman Trophy playing at USC two years before me. Mike wasn't having a very happy year up to that point. The Chiefs were alternating four running backs, and he wasn't getting as much chance to carry the ball as he would have liked. In addition, he had suffered through some ill feelings with some of his teammates. He had been appointed as head of a committee of players seeking better black housing in Kansas City; but after he went ahead and got a lot of publicity for the project, some of the other blacks seemed to back down. On the other hand, I had heard some of his teammates accuse him of giving up the cause himself. Whatever the reason, he wasn't feeling too satisfied. He was talking about sticking it out one more season so he would have five years and his pension. Then he hoped to retire and settle down in L.A. As it turned out, however, his good game against us was the first of many. He finished the season with a lot of solid games; maybe the Super Bowl victory and that big check mellowed his attitude about quitting.

"Don't get discouraged," Mike told me. "You've got a young team that's going to be very good some day. Just work hard and keep yourself healthy, so you'll be sure you're around when those good days arrive."

"I'm not too worried about staying healthy," I said. "I'm feeling more and more certain that those good days aren't too far away."

Chapter Fifteen

Getting Together

The night after the Kansas City game, most of us went to the Bills' annual Halloween party at Ron McDole's. I rented a Trojan costume and a toga so that Marquerite could go as Helen of Troy; we expected to have two of the most elaborate outfits, but we underestimated the effort everybody would put into their costumes. The party was full of weird sights. Waddey Harvey, a 280-pound defensive tackle, came as a hula dancer; tight end Billy Masters was a baby sucking a lollipop. The room was cluttered with ersatz hillbillies and hoboes, greasy garage mechanics and female impersonators—but undoubtedly the most believable costume belonged to Maguire, who came dressed as Captain Kangaroo. It was believable mainly because, with his round face and bushy mustache, Maguire would have looked a little like Captain Kangaroo even without a costume.

A Hollywood lot couldn't have built a better setting for a Halloween party. Ron and Paula McDole lived in a 150-year-old house in a town called Eden, way out in the country about forty miles from Buffalo. They had bought it when it was just an empty, creaking barn and fixed it up themselves. But even in its redecorated condition it was pretty spooky, a haunted house in the middle of nowhere. "If you fall off the back porch," said McDole, "we're not responsible for ever finding you."

Maguire spent most of the night telling stories about the people that had been murdered in the house and the curses that had been placed upon it. "The only reason McDole lives here," he said, "is that he's such a jealous husband. He knows that nobody would dare to mess with his wife out here because who could even think about sex in a place like this?" He said that McDole was cheap, too, and he always saved money on Halloween because the kids were too terrified to play trick-or-treat. In fact, he insisted that the first time the party had been held at McDole's, half of the players drove up the winding road to the house, took one look, and turned around to go home.

The mood was surprisingly good considering that we had lost not only the game, but also Guidry and Saimes. Guidry showed up fairly late with his arm in a sling and confirmed what we had already feared; his shoulder was separated and he was out for the season. Saimes didn't make it; he was back in the hospital awaiting surgery on his knee. Yet all the players seemed determined to enjoy themselves and stop feeling sorry for themselves as we had been doing for a few weeks.

As the drinks flowed and the music grew louder, the Bills seemed to move closer together than they had all year. It was the first time that the gap between the young and old members of the team didn't seem to exist. Our ages fell into an unusual pattern. There was a nucleus of veterans who had been through the Bills' best years and were now about thirty; the rest of the team seemed to consist almost entirely of rookies and second-year men. There was no middle group, made up of third- or fourth-

year players who might have identified with both the
older guys and the newcomers. So when we left the playing field, we would split into distinct social groups. Maguire was everybody's friend, but not too many other
friendships bridged the age gap.

At the party, however, no one seemed conscious of being young or old, black or white. We were simply a team,
dancing and singing, talking and horsing around in all
kinds of crazy ways, and a lot of guys got to know one
another for the first time. Whenever things were in
danger of slowing down, Maguire would pull another ridiculous stunt and get everybody laughing again. J.C. Collins
came dressed as a French chef, but Maguire told him
loudly, "You should have stuck a broomstick up your ass
and come as a fudgsicle. Then your wife could have come
as a vanilla wafer."

Paul Costa wore a priest's collar and a black suit with
a picture of Christ sticking out of the breast pocket. Fin-
gering a rosary, he announced that he was Father Hes-
burgh, president of Notre Dame, "and this is a picture of
my hippie cousin." He knew that his costume looked
authentic because he had stopped at a thruway toll booth
for directions and the toll collectors had said, "Right that
way, Father. Yes, Father. Have a good trip, Father."

"Oh f—— it," replied Paul. "I'm late for the party."

Later I got into a conversation with Costa about living
in Buffalo. Paul's wife Connie was making some remark
—the kind of thing everybody says about Buffalo—and
Paul cut her off. "We're here and there's nothing we can
do about it, and I don't think it does anybody any good
to complain about it all the time. After all, we're getting
paid to play a game for a living. That makes us luckier
than most people." He made his point. Marquerite and I
had reached the state where we were counting the days
until we could get back to California, but that really

wasn't helping us any. I decided that it was time I stopped wishing I was someplace else and began concentrating completely on doing my job in Buffalo.

Booker Edgerson hadn't bothered to wear a costume, but he was making his own contribution to the party by serving as official photographer. Booker is a camera fan and he has hundreds of dollars worth of equipment, but for the big event he had selected the camera he trusted most—a $6 Instamatic. Some of his candid shots wound up among the happiest mementos of the Bills' season.

I had classified Booker, who was thirty, as a member of the old guard on the Bills, and I hadn't expected to become too close to him. Yet as the season went on, we spent more and more time together, and I realized that when Booker is sixty, he will still be a young, open-minded guy. At first, his casual, almost uninterested attitude toward football had turned me off, but I later realized that he simply treated the game as what he thought it should be—a lot of fun. Booker didn't enjoy last season very much. "Coach Rauch has taken a lot of fun out of the game with his pregame check-ins at the hotel," he said. "When Lou Saban coached here, I had the feeling that he had more respect for the individuals on the club. We could do what we wanted and he trusted us to take care of ourselves. Rauch may have the right approach; maybe eventually the extra rules and procedures will help us win games. Maybe pro football isn't supposed to be that much fun. But right now I'd like to go back to the old way."

Off the field, Booker certainly didn't seem to be cutting down on his fun. He enjoyed his fast-paced life right in the middle of the city, hanging around the liveliest joints and becoming a local character. When I asked why he lived downtown, he said, "If I lived out where you guys live, instead of getting home at eight some mornings, I'd never get home at all. This way I feel more settled down."

When the old Bills had been winning titles, they had always been known as a tough, boisterous bunch of hell-raisers who won with sheer strength and enthusiasm. Watching McDole, Maguire, Sestak, and some of the other guys at the party, I could see that their reputation was deserved. They could have been a group of all-night truck-drivers, slugging down drinks and laughing and shouting. They were as tough and down-to-earth as their image; in some ways, they represented an old-fashioned group of football players. They had none of the glamour or public appeal that our generation has grown used to. They just did their jobs and took tremendous pride, as individuals and as a team, in what they accomplished.

Yet there were drawbacks to being that old-fashioned kind of player. At one point I was talking to Booker about the future. He said that the pace of his life would probably shorten his career. "But I'd rather play a few years less and enjoy it," he said, "than last until I'm thirty-six and live like a monk."

"What will you do when it's over?"

"I'm not sure," he said. "Maybe I'll continue the job I have with the phone company here, but more than likely, I'll go back to Rock Island, Illinois, and teach."

It gave me pause. Here was a man who had been one of the best cornerbacks in football for years, playing on championship teams. And when he retired, he would leave all the friendships and connections he had built up and go back to a little town to teach for $150 or $175 a week. "Won't it be hard to give up all the money and excitement you've gotten used to?" I asked him.

"What money? Football hasn't been such a big bonanza for me."

"You got a couple of championship checks."

"After taxes," he said, "my first championship check

came to under two thousand dollars. It must seem a long time ago to you, but there were times when we weren't exactly on top of the world. Maguire remembers a championship check that came to nine hundred dollars."

That was the generation gap in pro football. Since the big-money era had started with the war between the two leagues, many of us had been able to use bonuses and salaries to set up enterprises that would aid us throughout our lives. But for Booker and some of the others, football had simply been a job—something to enjoy and take pride in, but also something that would come to an end. Then it would be time to begin a new job. From that perspective, football didn't look like a very glamorous way of life. I didn't envy those guys when they finally had to finish their careers and start over in something else.

We all learned a little bit about one another that night. We began to see and understand things that might have been keeping us apart, and we left with a new feeling of unity. Briscoe had been right when he told the team that we should get together more, and we had taken a very enjoyable step in that direction. Only two players were noticeably absent, the nominal team leaders, Jacobs and Kemp.

It wouldn't have made much difference one way or another if Harry and Jack had been there, but their absence emphasized the fact that the younger guys were taking on more of a role in molding and leading the team. Veterans such as Maguire and McDole had always been outspoken and uninhibited; now many of us were beginning to feel just as free and open about things. It reflected what had happened the week before on the practice field. The young guys had been the ones who livened up the workouts; it had seemed to rub off on the veterans. Maybe that was what we needed all along—youthful eagerness. For all our mistakes, we had certainly shown it against

Kansas City for three quarters. If it kept growing, it might eventually carry us through a whole season.

For the first time in weeks, I plunged into our practice sessions with a vengeance. I couldn't wait to get out and hit somebody. Football seemed like fun again. Coach Rauch said that our Kansas City effort was as good as we'd had all year, and we all felt the same way. The press was criticizing Darragh severely and saying that Rauch should have put in Kemp late in the game when the Chiefs were mauling Dan. But the players had respected Darragh's effort and his guts. We were sure that as his arm got stronger and his timing improved, he could lead us to some victories. With a 2-6 record, we couldn't afford to dream of dramatic winning streaks and post-season playoffs. But we could be spoilers, and we could finish the year on a crest that would carry us at full speed into the next season. The first team we had a chance to knock off was New York.

The weather was cold and rainy and people talked about the beginning of the snowy season in Buffalo, but our mood remained enthusiastic. Everybody was fighting hard in practice and joking afterwards. The tensions of the past weeks had turned into determination, and at last we seemed to have a confident, winning attitude. I felt really comfortable with all the other Bills, and the rest of the young guys were getting the same feeling. Robert James and Wayne Patrick were two prime examples. They no longer smiled shyly and tried to stay in the background; a few good games and the new spirit on the club had made them as outgoing as anybody on the team. They had won everybody's respect. In fact, some of the older guys wanted to campaign for the institution of an All-AFL specialty team because Robert James would have been a unanimous selection.

In our first game against the Jets I had carried the ball only ten times. With Darragh at quarterback, I was sure I would get it more often and do better than the 35 yards I made on opening day. And I was confident that the feeling that carried us through three quarters against the Chiefs could sustain us all the way in New York.

I did get the ball a little more, and I gained 70 yards in fourteen carries. Our attitude also held up, and our defense was even better than it had been against Kansas City. But we lost, 16-6, in what had to be our unluckiest game of the season.

Luck in football is often directly related to how well you play. A team that's winning tends to make its own breaks, while a loser brings bad luck on itself. When we suffered key fumbles or penalties in some of our early games, I had to admit that we were bringing a lot of the trouble on ourselves. But against the Jets, we were really snakebit. I saw the kind of day it would be on our first series. Darragh picked the Jets apart, hitting Briscoe and Masters with good passes and giving me the ball for a 14-yard run; we quickly drove from our twenty-three to the Jet three. On our second try, I scored. But when I was already on the ground in the end zone, I saw the official drop his flag. He was calling me—incredibly late— for having been in motion too soon. I'll argue that call until I die; I was sure he was wrong then, and was even more convinced after I watched the films. But the decision had been made, we lost the touchdown, and moments later Bruce Alford even had a 13-yard field goal blocked. We had shoved them down the field and the score was still 0-0.

We played the same way all afternoon. Darragh was leading us very well, our defense was giving Namath a hard time, and we outgained and outplayed them. Yet in five drives to within 20 yards of the Jets' goal line, we managed to net a total of 6 points. It was only a matter of time before our generosity caught up with us, and two more tremendous breaks gave the Jets the edge they needed. The first came when Namath threw a pass to the goal line toward Maynard, who appeared to be covered perfectly by Booker. Joe threw it harmlessly over Maynard's head, but the official called interference and gave them the ball on the one. Then they scored their only touchdown to take a 7-0 lead.

The biggest blow came minutes later. Darragh had us moving again when he released a screen pass just as Verlon Biggs and Gerry Philbin crashed into him. Dan didn't get up, and I got a sick feeling. We had waited all year hoping to find a leader for our offense, and now, after less than two full games, he lay crumpled on the ground. Darragh, who had completed eight of ten passes for 152 yards, left the game with a dislocated shoulder; he didn't play again all season.

Kemp came in and we continued to move the ball. Then Jack had to scramble to the Jet thirty-six, Larry Grantham nailed him as he went out of bounds. Kemp was groggy; Briscoe replaced him. Marlin hadn't worked at quarterback since joining the Bills, but he stepped up to the line of scrimmage with his usual brash confidence. He faked a handoff to me, rolled to his right, and appeared ready to break away on one of those wild runs he used to make at Denver. But Marlin suddenly saw Bubba Thornton open across the field. And in his rare chance at quarterback, he wasn't about to run if he had a man open for a pass. He threw, misjudging the distance slightly. The ball hung in the air in front of Bubba just long enough for Billy Baird to step in at the Jet seven-yard-line for the interception.

While our offense stumbled, our defense kept us close;

two field goals by Jim Turner put the Jets ahead, 13-6, midway in the last quarter, but we still had a good chance. At that point I received one of the most pleasant surprises of the season; instead of going pass-crazy, Kemp seemed determined to stay on the ground. He gave me the ball twice in a row and I got decent yardage. Then, on my third straight try, I stumbled. My foot slipped out from under me at the snap of the ball, and I was still off-balance as Jack turned to slap the ball into my chest. It hit my shoulder pad and bounced free before I could grab it. John Neidert recovered the loose ball for the Jets and our last hope faded. It was one of the season's more ironic moments. At last Jack had given me a chance to do the job myself—and I had to pick that moment to lose my footing.

The mood in the locker room was surprisingly good. For the second week in a row, we had fought one of the best teams in the league down to the final minutes. Once again the defense had every reason to be proud of itself; and even our offense had shown an ability to move the ball, at least until we penetrated the twenty-yard-line. Bad luck and all, we knew that it was a game we could have won. There was no longer a wide gulf between teams like the Chiefs and Jets and our club. Despite our 2-7 record and our costly mistakes at crucial moments, we were at last acting and thinking like a real football team.

Mike Battle had a big party that night in his East Side apartment. A lot of the Bills went with me, and a number of Mike's friends on the Jets also showed up. Mike was on top of the world. He had not only fooled all his critics by making the team, but he had become an important part of the New York club, both on and off the field. He returned punts and kickoffs, was the Jets' answer to

Robert James on their kicking and punting teams, and had high hopes of eventually breaking into the lineup at safety. He was also a fast-growing legend in New York. As soon as they entered the apartment, a few of the Jets came up to me and said, "Was Battle always this crazy?"

He *had* been, of course, and he wasn't slowing down a bit. He had moved in right alongside Namath among New York's most sought-after bachelors, and he was full of tales of beautiful women sending limousines for him at all hours. Once he poured me a glass of champagne, then hit my arm accidentally, and spilled some of it. He tried to fill it again, but somebody else bumped into me. "That's a bad glass," he announced, grabbing it from my hand and throwing it out the window. He listened to it crash on the pavement eleven floors below and turned to the bartender. "This time," he said, "give O.J. a steadier glass. And a bigger one. He needs to make up for lost time."

Most of us spent the night milling around, laughing and getting to know people. But two athletes were noticeably quiet, standing near a corner of the room talking strictly business. Butch Byrd and George Sauer probably studied the game of football as carefully as any two men who played it, and their long-standing rivalry was as mental as it was physical. Butch had been covering Sauer for five seasons; while George was always near the top of the pass receivers' standings, he had seldom had much success against Butch. In our two games last season, Sauer had only one catch—and that came in the game in New York on a play when both Harry Jacobs and Pete Richardson blitzed and Namath read it perfectly.

As usual, Butch's success against Sauer was based as much on strategy as on physical ability. Butch had burned Namath with key interceptions several times over the years. Joe knew that Butch was willing to gamble in an effort to pick one off, and he usually didn't think it was worth the gamble to throw in his direction. In fact, George told him that Joe would almost never risk a sideline pass against him because Butch was so adept at timing the ball and grabbing it to go in for an easy touchdowns. Sauer and Byrd spent much of the night discussing patterns and tactics; it was obvious that they enjoyed talking shop as much as many athletes enjoyed getting away from thoughts of their sport. They were two professionals, and the unique battle that goes on between a receiver and a cornerback had produced a great mutual respect between them.

Toward the end of the night things began getting a little wild. Battle went out for extra ice, hurdling every fire hydrant on the street on his way to his neighborhood bar. Then he came back mad because the guys in the bar had laughed when somebody said he was Mike Battle. No one believed that such a skinny kid could have been a football player. Some of the people at the party were just as mad; some guys I didn't know had begun to look for trouble. There were a few confrontations and angry words, but things eventually blew over and nobody became too upset. After all, it wouldn't have seemed like a Mike Battle party if somebody hadn't tried to start a brawl.

I stayed in New York on Monday for one of those exhausting "days off" that I was coming to expect. I had to sign some contracts with Chuck, pose for some pictures for a magazine spread, and meet with Mike Rathet of the Associated Press, who wanted to do a big two-part piece on how my rookie year was going. Then I went up to a studio to tape the *Joe Namath Show*. A goofy blonde introduced the guests, actor Maximilian Schell and me. Then she said that Schell had played

Hamlet three times and I had played the Jets twice. "I hope," she added, "that Schell did better against Hamlet than Simpson did against the Jets."

Flying back to Buffalo, I thought about all the media people who had surrounded me in New York. At times during the year all the attention had become a little tiring; at some of the lowest moments, I had actually envied some of the other guys who were allowed to get dressed and get out of sight as quickly as possible. Yet the constant motion and excitement of New York had also reminded me how lucky I was. We were a second-division team, I was far down in the rushing statistics, and it would have been very easy for people to start calling me a big flop in pro football. Instead, everyone seemed to be giving me the benefit of the doubt. They still wanted to see and hear me, and they seemed to share my own conviction that sooner or later I would begin making up for my slow start as a pro. So I had no complaints at all about being besieged for interviews and appearances in New York. I wouldn't have wanted it any other way.

Chapter Sixteen

A Feeling of Pride

To an outsider it may sound silly to claim that the attitude on the Bills was undergoing important changes. We were still a losing club, and worse yet, we hadn't even scored a touchdown in our last three games. To many observers, there were few reasons to suspect that things were improving. Yet in the minds of the players, the team that prepared for our return match with the Miami Dolphins bore little resemblance to the tense and bitter group that had filed mournfully from the locker room only three weeks earlier after that pitiful defeat. Our good efforts against the Chiefs and Jets had something to do with the change, but the real transformation was more subtle. We were no longer rookies and veterans, offense and defense—separate groups ready to point the finger at someone else for everything that went wrong. We were a unit, ready to win or lose together, and confident that we would be doing a lot more winning than losing.

Early in the season it had often seemed that Maguire was the only one who could talk freely to everyone. The rest of us tended to be guarded about our ideas and opinions; nobody was sure just how much talking would be accepted by the rest of the team. But after nine games we felt comfortable enough to say almost anything. In fact, we may have been a little too comfortable because several of our comments found their way into print. Yet those incidents—which might have caused trouble weeks before—blew over, a fact which indicated how far we had come.

The biggest storm broke over a column in which Haven Moses was quoted as saying that everybody knew that Jack Kemp was over the hill. When I arrived for our Tuesday meetings, I saw Coach Rauch talking to Haven off in a corner. When Haven came over to me, I asked him what was going on, but he wouldn't talk about it. Max Anderson filled me in on what had happened and told me that Haven had flatly denied making the statement. We wondered how Kemp would react to it, but when Jack arrived he didn't say anything; no one had shown him the article yet.

It could have been a tense scene, but it turned into just the opposite. I was the one who started the kidding about it. "Hey Jack," I called, "don't get upset about what Haven said about you. He didn't know the writer was going to print it." Jack looked at Haven, who didn't know what to say.

"I told you, Haven," I went on, "never tell writers what you really believe unless you expect them to print it."

"What are you talking about?" asked Jack—and everybody broke up. Somebody told him about the article and he looked at Haven again. For a moment he pretended to be mad; then he and Haven both laughed along with us. We were starting practice at a new field that day, and on the bus ride to the field, we never let up on Haven. Every time he opened his mouth somebody would shout, "Don't tell that to the press." When we reached the field, Haven and Jack walked off the bus together; it appeared that there were no hard feelings. When they kept talking for a while, we all got on Haven again and told him to stop Bud Jonesing.

Then we turned our attention to Charley Ferguson, Charley was celebrating his thirtieth birthday that week, and we started kidding him that he was the oldest taxi squad player in history. Charley had been unlucky throughout his career. He had tried out with Cleveland and Minnesota before coming to Buffalo; after two good years as the Bills' tight end, he had missed the 1967 season with an ankle injury—and he had spent two more years trying to fight his way back into action. The coaches must have seen something in him in order to keep him around; yet here he was thirty years old and nearing the end of his career, and he hadn't gotten into a game in three years. Every week or so he would talk about getting activated, but it didn't look as if it were ever going to happen. So in practice, every time he caught a pass, we all yelled, "Charley Ferguson—a game check this week for Charley Ferguson."

I was the next target for the needling. For about the 988th time, one of the papers had an article about how I wasn't getting the ball enough. Those articles were starting to get a little boring, and I knew that some readers probably got the wrong impression from them. My stand on the matter was simple. As long as it was for the good of the team, I would be happy to be a decoy, a blocker, a receiver, or anything else. But that strategy hadn't been working very well and as long as we weren't winning, I thought that the team might as well try to give me the ball. I knew that I'd made mistakes and failed to run as well as I could have in some games; but I still had trouble accepting the fact that I was averaging about fifteen carries a game. On every team I had ever played for, if we got behind, I was sure to get the ball more. In Buffalo, when we fell behind it seemed to lessen my chances of getting it. And being a running back, I would have been crazy not to want to run with the ball. I had never lied to the press before, and I couldn't see lying when they asked me if I wished to carry the ball more. I wasn't unhappy, I wasn't mad at anybody; but when people asked, I told them that I'd prefer to run more. Who wouldn't?

Nevertheless, the guys wanted to give back some of the flack that I'd been giving them, and the latest article gave them the opportunity. "Give O.J. the ball," they called in practice. "He wants the ball, so we'd better give it to him." The writer had quoted me as saying, "When the Chicago Bears get behind, you can be sure that they're going to give the ball to Gale Sayers."

"You're right about the Bears, O.J.," said Maguire. "But we don't *have* a Gale Sayers to give the ball to."

It was mid-November and in Buffalo, that means winter. We switched our workouts from the stadium and Houghton Park to a wide-open field called Sheridan Park. We moved partly to solve our persistent spy problem, but it didn't help much. When we arrived for our first day there, a fair-sized group of fans was already waiting for us. "We could go to the Sahara Desert," said Bob Lustig, the team's general manager, "and a camel caravan would come along and find us."

"What I don't understand," said Coach Rauch, "is what enjoyment they get out of standing in the freezing cold, watching something that, to them, has to seem pretty dull."

Park officials put up a temporary fence to keep the observers pretty far away, but a spy would still have been able to see what we were doing. A number of kids easily scrambled over the fence to get a closer look. One of them even rushed up to Bugsy Engelberg to ask for a tryout as a placekicker. After Alford's bad day in New York, half the fans in Buffalo probably thought that they could improve our field goal kicking. Bugsy let the kid try and he really boomed a few; unfortunately, none of them came within ten yards of the goal posts.

Even if it didn't cut down the audience, the shift to Sheridan Park certainly lowered the temperature for the workouts. The field was good, but it was out near Lake Erie and there wasn't a building in sight to block the wind. It howled off the lake and across that big flat plain, and I was as cold as I'd ever been in my life. And shortly after we arrived out there, it started to snow. This was the image I had always had of playing football in a place like Buffalo; I was glad that, for most of the season, it hadn't come true.

Late in the week the snow became heavier and we moved indoors, into a rickety building that was also a horse stable and riding area. It wasn't much warmer than it had been outside, but at least the wind didn't roar through it quite as badly—and for once, we knew there were no spies around. There was also no football field. The building was long enough, but it was only about 20 yards wide; it felt like we were running our plays in a tunnel. Yet the bizarre surroundings only added to the team's high spirits. The long bus rides from the stadium —where we'd get into uniform—got funnier each day. Even the coaches would spend half the trip laughing at all the wisecracks. At the stable, guys on the sidelines picked up frozen pieces of manure and started throwing them around. We ran through our drills crisply and enthusiastically; we had to move fast just to keep warm.

Both Bob Griese and Nick Buoniconti of the Dolphins were injured, and there were reports that they might miss the game. I had mixed feelings about it. I knew that my chances of running well would improve with Buoniconti

out, but I also wanted to prove that we could whip the
Dolphins when they were at full strength. I felt that my
running had improved sharply since our first game against
them, and I was hoping for a chance to throw some
moves at Buoniconti and make him pay for the job he
had done on me the first time around.

On the night before the game, we were supposed to
check into Michael's Inn up in Canada again. The coach
still felt that there were too many distractions around the
Fairfax in Buffalo. It was a funny thought: Too many
distractions in the city of Buffalo.

We were due at 6:30, but a few hours earlier, the snow
really started to come down. I left the apartment early,
planning to allow plenty of time for driving in the snow;
but I wasn't used to how bad winter-driving could be in
the North. Inching along the winding road toward Canada
in my little Corvette, I was really scared. The snow was
so thick that I couldn't see the road, the lights, anything.
If I had gone as fast as 20 miles per hour, I was sure
the car would spin out of control. I couldn't even make
out any tire tracks in front of me that I could follow, and
I had no idea which side of the road I was on. A few
times I thought I would definitely crack up. At one point
I thought about pulling over to the side and parking; but I
figured that it wouldn't take long for the car to be buried
under the snow, and then I'd never get out of there. Finally,
through the driving snow, I was able to see the highway
lights hit the road near the middle of my side of the
highway. So I just got right under the lights and stayed
there. After what seemed like six hours, I made it to
Michael's Inn.

Everybody made it eventually, although a lot of the
guys were hours late. Booker's wife drove up to drop him
off and decided to stay there rather than risk the trip
back. I even wondered how we would manage to get

back the next morning for the game. It was a little ridiculous, really. Here we had a game scheduled a few miles away from our homes, and we had to spend the night before it battling a blizzard to go twenty miles further away.

They were used to snowstorms up there, however, and the next morning I was surprised to see how well the streets had been cleared. We all took off early and got home with no trouble. We spent an hour digging some of the guys' cars from under the drifts, and then made it to the stadium in plenty of time. The playing conditions were amazing. After two weeks of rain and snow, I had expected it to be a mess. But the ground crew had the snow piled along the sidelines, and the field itself was in fine shape. It was, in fact, a beautiful day for the game.

The first three plays of the game gave me my best moments of the entire year. We received the opening kickoff, and had a reverse planned. When Bubba or I took the kick, we were supposed to start upfield and give it to Hilton Crawford on the reverse. I caught the ball and started forward, looking for Hilton; he wasn't anywhere in sight. I later learned that he had lined up on the wrong side of the field. By the time it dawned on me that he wasn't going to take the ball, several tacklers were bearing down on me. I accelerated quickly and burst past the first wave, broke a few more tackles, and spun into the clear. I should have gone all the way, but I was tripped up from behind after making 73 yards.

I got caught because I was stumbling. I had just broken away from what I thought was the last man, and I was still trying to straighten up and turn it on again when somebody hit me. Unfortunately for me, the guy happened to be a linebacker, Jess Powell; I didn't hear the end of that for weeks. The night before, we had been looking at some films in which Floyd Little got caught from behind on a long run. I'd said that if I ever got caught from behind, I'd buy drinks for everybody on the team. The first time I returned to the sideline, Billy Shaw started laughing about it. Not only had I been caught, but I had been caught by a big old linebacker. Billy promised me that I'd never live it down.

Buoniconti's bad knee had kept him out of the game, as expected, but it didn't take me long to meet his replacement, Frank Emanuel. On our first play from scrimmage, I ran a flare pattern out of the backfield. I hesitated until the middle opened up, then moved across into the open area. I got a step on Emanuel and was free for a pass, but he chased me and clotheslined me from behind. It was an illegal play, and if the referee had seen him, he would have drawn a penalty; in fact, when Harry Jacobs had been penalized for hitting Ron Sellers of the Patriots on a similar play, the league office had even fined him. Emanuel's forearm almost took my helmet off, and I was knocked completely off balance; but as I stumbled forward, Kemp saw me in the clear and threw the ball. I managed to catch it and stumble down to the eight-yard-line for an 18-yard gain.

On the next play, I was sent in motion; my assignment was basically to draw a defender out of the play and keep him there. But when I got out there, I saw that Jack was in trouble. The primary receiver was covered and Jack was scrambling, looking for someone else. So I hooked back over the middle and he drilled a pass right into my chest for the touchdown. The little things that had so often gone wrong for us were at last turning out right; I knew then that we were finally going to put together a solid all-around game.

In his first start since our first Miami disaster, Kemp called his plays brilliantly. He passed well, avoided the interceptions that had hurt us so much—and kept going back to the running game. We ran well—I gained 72 yards in twenty-one carries—and controlled the ball on a number of drives. Our defensive linemen seemed to appreciate the extra rest we gave them on the bench, and really blasted in on the pass rush. They were aided, of course, by the absence of Griese since substitute Rick Norton was often slow in getting rid of the ball. But they still deserved tremendous credit for the pressure they put on Norton; in fact, their effort was reminiscent of what the Chiefs had done to Darragh two weeks earlier. They nailed Norton eight times for 83 yards—and their biggest tackles came when the Dolphins were moving deep into our territory.

Maguire played a role in our second touchdown. Our drive stalled and Paul went in to punt, but he was brushed by an onrushing lineman as he kicked the ball. There wasn't really much contact, but Paul went into a magnificent backward swan dive and drew a penalty call. Awarded the ball back, we went on to score. Meanwhile, the kind of nightmares that usually happened to us were killing Miami. Trailing 14-3, the Dolphins moved to our five-yard-line, and then receiver Larry Seiple shook free in the end zone—only to have Norton's pass hit the crossbar and bounce harmlessly away.

Our defense was not as technically perfect as it had been for two weeks; it yielded more yards and made a few more mistakes. But on both offense and defense, we were making the big plays that had been eluding us in other games. Once, for example, Mercury Morris hesitated at the line and then shot past linebacker Edgar Chandler, who was doing a great job filling in for Guidry. Edgar was beaten on the play and Mercury caught a 23-yard pass; but Chandler caught up to him and hit him so hard that he fumbled. Booker picked it up and

ran it back to the Dolphin nineteenth to set up another
score.

In the fourth quarter I made one of my few poor
plays in the game. Running a pattern over the middle,
I reached for a pass that was a little low, started to run
before I had a grip on the ball, and dropped it. But on
the next play I ran the same play and Jack hit me. I
sprinted toward the sideline as Haven and Marlin rushed
over to screen off some tacklers; then I turned and raced
toward the end zone. The play covered 55 yards and
put a very satisfying victory on ice, 28-3.

With about a minute to go, Rauch put Maguire in
at linebacker. It was the first time all year that Paul
had played on anything but special teams, and he was
really funny. When he took his position, he looked around
as if he were in a strange country; on the sidelines, we
all laughed and wondered if he would know what the
hell to do. And the man he would have to cover on pass
plays was Mercury Morris, one of the fastest backs in
football. The Dolphins only ran one play to his side.
Morris ran a pattern, but the ball was thrown low and
as it landed on the ground, Maguire sprawled all over it.
The game ended a few seconds later, and Paul came off
the field and said, "Well, I shut my man out."

It was Kemp's best performance since the Denver
game, and I thought that it was even better because
he had never let himself get carried away with passing.
He was surrounded by reporters afterward, and Maguire
yelled, "Give them some of those big words of yours,
Jack. They won't know what they mean or how to spell
them."

A lot of people asked me if we would have done as well
against the Miami defense if Buoniconti had played. It
was a question that no one could really have answered.
Of course they would have been a little tougher with

him in there. But when you're on the field, you're not conscious of what one defender might be doing or what somebody else would have done in his place. We had mixed our plays and executed much better than we had in Miami, and we had avoided the costly penalties that had hurt us the first time we played the Dolphins. With all those improvements, I was sure that we would have whipped them regardless of who had been playing. In fact, for three weeks in a row, we had played well enough to give anybody a battle. The Buffalo fans went a little overboard when they immediately started talking about a playoff spot for us. We were still only 3-7 and would need a great streak to catch second-place Houston. But playoffs or not, we could at last walk out of the locker room and through the caverns under the stadium with a feeling of pride in being the Buffalo Bills.

Chapter Seventeen

"O. J. Who?"

The week before our game in Boston, there was a lot of talk about who would be Rookie of the Year. Somebody interviewed Ron Sellers, the Patriots' wide receiver, and Sellers gave his estimate of the rookies' race. He thought that his teammate Carl Garrett was in the lead, with Cincinnati quarterback Greg Cook in second. And he added that he gave himself a pretty good shot at it, too. A lot of the Bills got a kick out of that because up to that point, Sellers had only caught about a dozen passes. Some of the guys started kidding me about it. They said that if the Patriots were going to start advertising their own contenders, maybe the Bills should start lobbying for me.

Actually, the Rookie-of-the-Year situation had been the farthest thing from my mind. I had assumed that I was way out of the running after all the bad games I had played. But when the other players started talking about it, I looked around and found to my surprise that there just wasn't anyone who was having a really outstanding first year. I had missed one game, carried ten times or less in three others, and suffered through terrible afternoons such as that first Miami game. Yet I was eighth in the AFL in rushing, and my 73-yard return against Miami had put me into the lead in kickoff returns. People seemed to think that I would battle Garrett and Cook for the rookie award—and that our next two games would provide head-on comparisons with both of them.

It didn't really work out that way. Garrett got a big break in our game in Boston, breaking loose for a long touchdown run when they were just running out the clock; that boosted his statistics, but in whatever personal battle we were having, I didn't think that either of us gained a clear edge. Then we played Cincinnati in a snowstorm that hindered my running and made it virtually impossible for Cook to throw—so that didn't prove anything, either. In any case, it seemed strange to be approaching the end of what was basically a disappointing season and to still find myself in consideration for any kind of title at all.

The temperature in Buffalo was dropping steadily. It seemed to snow more every day—except on the days when we got freezing rain. Somebody told me that it was the worst early winter anyone could remember in Buffalo, although I had a feeling that Buffalonians always said things like that to visitors from California. (It turned out that the guy was right; the winter set a record for snowfall in Buffalo, but luckily I only had to read about the last 50 inches or so from a safe distance in Los Angeles.) But we had a lively week of practice, most of it in that horse stable, and we had good reason to think we would beat the Patriots. Actually, it was an interesting confrontation. We were 3-7 and they were 2-8, and yet both clubs had been playing extremely well for the last month or so.

After missing my first shot at them, I was anxious to run against the Patriots; Wayne Patrick, who had enjoyed such a great game against them, was just as enthusiastic. Wingate had missed the Miami game with a bruised ankle that he had suffered against the Jets, but during our workouts he won his job back from Bill Enyart. Bill had run well against Miami, but the coaches evidently thought that Wingate was just a step quicker. Wingate and Bill were an engaging pair, both smiling and laughing as they spent the entire year fighting for one job. Enyart had been nicknamed Earthquake in college when he was a workhorse fullback for Oregon State. Nobody in Buffalo called him Earthquake, but Maguire soon started calling him Tremor. Bill, as usual, just giggled and said, "Aw, Paul . . ."

One morning that week I picked up the paper and got a jolt. Mike Taylor, my good friend from USC, had been put on waivers by the Steelers. I could hardly believe it because I knew he had started almost every game for them at offensive tackle. But Pittsburgh had been losing every week and I guess the coach was desperately trying to shake up the team—so Mike was let go. The official reason was that he had a weight problem.

He called me the same night and said, "Man, they did it to me."

"How could they do that?"

"They could, and they did." Mike was bitter about it. But I could understand how it could have happened. Mike was a very stubborn, strong-willed guy, and he had trouble getting along with a lot of people. He didn't know how to accept a statement he disagreed with and just keep quiet. When he thought that he was getting a bad deal, he had to let everybody know about it. He told me that when things got really bad—which they naturally did, on a team that finished 1-13—the coaches pointed to him as one of the main causes. And he didn't hesitate to tell them what he thought of their opinions. Whatever he said must have been strong because they didn't even bother to bench him and try to trade him. They cut him and placed him immediately on waivers.

I told Coach Rauch about Mike the next day, and he was very interested. "He was with you at USC in 1967, wasn't he?"

"Yeah, we were national champions and he was drafted in the first round," I said. "He has the potential to become a top pro tackle." I wasn't just saying nice things about a friend. I knew that when Mike really dedicated himself to his job, he could be as good as almost anybody. And apparently Rauch had also been impressed by him.

"But there isn't a thing I can do," the coach said, "unless he clears waivers in the NFL first. If he does, then I definitely want to talk to him." Unfortunately, Mike didn't clear the waivers. Both New Orleans and Minnesota put in bids, and he went to New Orleans, where he played one game and then finished the season on the taxi squad. Coach Rauch didn't forget our conversation, however. Several times he asked me how Mike was doing, giving me some hope that he might eventually make a deal for him if it was possible.

I was glad the coach was interested, and not only because I would have loved to play with Mike again. A few months earlier in the season, I wouldn't have dared to approach Rauch with a suggestion about a player. Like most of the younger players, I had considered him a cold and distant figure who would resent any unsolicited comment from a rookie. Yet over a period of a few weeks, we had begun to feel much closer to the coach. The fact that the team was playing well had something to do with it; his methods were much easier to appreciate when we could see the results on the field. And the bus rides to Sheridan Park had also broken a lot of barriers. When all the joking was at its height, the coach smiled and made a few wry comments himself. In his quiet way, he showed us that he shared many of our own feelings. Without even thinking about it, we had all stopped using the nickname Satan.

The game was played in Newton, Massachusetts, on the Boston College field—one of several temporary homes that the Patriots had used while waiting to get a new stadium built, or to move to another city. The small stands were packed, and many fans had banners begging the Patriots to stay in town. The game must have made a lot of them even more determined to keep the team. It was hard-hitting, wide-open, and exciting—and unfortunately for us, the Patriots closed their home season with a 35-21 victory.

We had begun to take our superb defense for granted, expecting it to keep games close while the offense made mistakes and tried to get going. But even a defense as good as ours probably figured to have a letdown at some point—and it happened that afternoon in Boston. To make it more ironic, we had our best offensive game of the year, statistically, rolling up a total of 432 yards. But Jack abandoned the steady play-calling he had given us the week before, went a little pass-crazy, and threw four interceptions; and for once, our defense wasn't able to keep our rivals from taking advantage of each break.

The game illustrated one fact that some fans may have tended to overlook; no players were more vital to us—or to any good defensive team—than the cornerbacks. Week after week, we counted on Butch to keep receivers and quarterbacks off balance with his daring plays and interceptions, while Booker covered his man like a blanket and batted down every pass that came his way. Yet in Boston, Butch allowed two long touchdown passes from Mike Taliaferro to Charley Frazier, and Booker gave up five receptions and one touchdown to Sellers. That meant 21 points that we didn't ordinarily figure to give up, and we couldn't make up the difference on offense.

I had a good day running, with 98 yards in seventeen carries; Wingate added 39 yards rushing and caught eight swing passes for another 59. But the Patriots struck for some quick touchdowns, and Jack went more and more to his passing to get us out of the hole. He had a strange day. He completed eighteen of thirty-two for 255 yards, often drilling the ball beautifully or hitting receivers long. But he made four really poor passes and each one was picked off; one led to the first Boston score, and two others killed our drives deep in their territory.

My most satisfying play came in the second period. I ran a sweep to the right for 6 yards before two guys grabbed me by the legs. As I was starting to go down, I saw a third defender—linebacker John Bramlett—sailing toward me. I had been waiting for Bramlett. When he had played for Miami the year before, he had been the man who ruined Ben Gregory's knee. Then, in Buffalo, he had broken Max Anderson's jaw. Ben and Max had been talking about him before the game. They said that he wasn't too big, but he was tough—and he had a tendency to hit late. "Just keep an eye on him," Ben had told me—and then I found my eyes right on him as he came up to take a late shot at me.

He apparently thought that I was on my way down and wouldn't see him, so he put his head down and charged. I dug in and threw a shoulder into him. I really popped him. He went down hard and lay there for a minute. Then he struggled to his feet and staggered to the sideline like a drunk. He didn't return until late in the game and when he did, he never got another shot at me. "Beautiful," Ben said on the sideline. "You gave a little of his crap back to him."

It was a rugged game all around. Once Kemp scrambled for some yardage and was knocked out of bounds by several Boston linemen. Even when Jack was on the ground and far out of bounds, one of their guys tried to drive him back into our bench. A fight broke out, but it ended before any real punches were thrown. Afterwards one of the Boston writers asked defensive end Larry Eisenhauer what had happened. "Oh, it was nothing much," he said, "Coach Rauch was trying to hit Jack Kemp. We were trying to pull them apart.

Carl Garrett had a fine game, especially returning kicks. He went 63 yards with a kickoff and 41 with a punt; but as the end of the game approached, I still had about twice as many rushing yards as he did. Then, on a routine off-tackle play designed to run out the clock, he slipped away from our linemen and raced 44 yards for a touchdown. The fans went wild, and in the section behind our bench, they started a loud chant, "O.J. Who? O.J. Who?" It was pretty funny, and they kept it up until the clock ran out.

I walked off the field with Carl and congratulated him on the year he was having. He had been drafted in the third round from a little school called New Mexico Highlands; shortly after he signed he had announced, "I'm going to beat out O.J. for Rookie of the Year." At that point, it appeared that he had made his prediction come true. When Billy Sullivan, the Patriots' owner, stopped in our locker room to meet me, I couldn't resist teasing him a little because I knew that he had a reputation for being even tougher about money than Mr. Wilson had been with me. "Garrett's a great player," I told him.

"He certainly is," he said with a big smile.

"You ought to give him a huge raise."

The smile became a litle bit frozen. "Yes," he said. "We're thinking about it."

I had to fly to New York that night to do an ABC interview with Steve Owens of Oklahoma, who was the favorite to win the Heisman Trophy. I rode the team bus to the Boston airport, and happened to sit across from Coach Rauch and his wife. The coach wasn't in a good mood, but he didn't seem too upset about the game. We had a long conversation, mostly about college football. I was feeling more comfortable with him each time we got together.

Ralph Wilson was on the plane I took to New York. I hadn't spoken to him too often during the season, except at our postgame parties when there were always other people who wanted to see him. During our negotiations, I had thought of him as a pretty cold character, but he turned out to be a very friendly man. We exchanged ideas on what the Bills needed for the future, and he asked me a lot of questions about my business projects, especially with Chevrolet. "Any time I can be of help," he said, "don't hesitate to come to me."

I realized that once a player became a part of his team, Mr. Wilson took a real interest in him. After all our fights over my contract, he was still anxious to do anything he could for me. He also told me some of Cookie Gilchrist's wild financial schemes—uranium mines and other strange ventures. He was a very witty story-teller and the trip passed quickly. In New York, we decided to share a cab into the city. But the first cab driver who pulled up to us was one of those creeps that you always seem to find at New York airports on busy Sunday nights. He snarled, "I won't take ya if you're going to two different places." I wasn't sure if he was trying to avoid taking a black man who might want to go to Harlem, or if he was just trying to rob us of as much extra money as he could; with New York cab drivers, it's hard to separate one gripe from another. But Mr. Wilson finally told him to get lost and signaled the next cab that came along. The first guy hadn't known what he was missing. For a $7 fare, Wilson gave our driver a $20 bill and didn't ask for change. "Maybe I should be driving you around in cabs," I told him. "I'll make more money than I did negotiating a contract with you."

Chapter Eighteen

Goodbye, Buffalo

If nothing else, the weather for our last game in Buffalo made me happier than ever to be getting out of town. When people tell cruel jokes about how frozen and barren Buffalo can be, they are accurately describing the week of our final home game against Cincinnati. Since we would be finishing the season with road games in Kansas City and San Diego, Marquerite went directly home to L.A. that week. And as the snow swirled against the windows of the apartment, I often wished that I were going with her.

Marquerite had assembled an amazing amount of clothing in her few months in Buffalo, and when it was time to pack her stuff, I had to buy an extra trunk. Somebody advised me to go to a bargain store in the ghetto; I inched my way through the snow until I found the store, and was greeted by a white salesman who had one of the classic ghetto-store sales pitches. It took him about ten minutes to describe all the wonders of a very ordinary-looking trunk. Then he told me that he could give it to me for the special bargain price of $27. It was a special *ghetto* bargain price, I soon learned; the same trunk was sold in the suburbs for $22. I paid the $27 and was glad just to get back home and out of the storm. But as always, I was annoyed at the way the black people downtown were being victimized. Similar hustlers operated, of course, in Watts and every other ghetto. Yet the problem had struck me as more flagrant during my stay in Buffalo. Blacks seemed to me to accept injustices more calmly in the East. Perhaps because of the existence of a more stable middle class in places like Baldwin Hills in L.A., I felt that blacks demanded—and got— more respect in the West. I hoped that people such as the blacks who had thrown the party for the team would gradually achieve that kind of respect in Buffalo, and I made up my mind to help them achieve it as my career went on.

I had trouble renting a station wagon to take our trunks to the airport, but a local Chevrolet dealer finally helped me out, and Ben and I mucked through the snow and ice and got everything on its way. Marquerite took some of my stuff home, but I left a lot of it with Ben, who was planning to spend the off-season in Buffalo. It was a funny feeling, leaving so many of my belongings behind me; it made the idea sink in that, for better or worse, Buffalo would be my part-time home for a long time to come.

As bad as the weather was, the mood of the team kept improving. The barriers that had separated us from the coaching staff for much of the year had finally been eliminated. Coach Rauch joined in more and more of our kidding, and the guys who had grumbled about him the most were speaking of him with increasing respect. In addition, we were getting to know and like some of the assistants. One in particular became a regular part of our relaxed routine during practices—Claude (Hoot) Gibson, the defensive backfield coach. Hoot was only thirty, but he acted as if he were twenty-one and his own career were beginning all over again. He had starred at North Carolina State and then played defense and returned kicks for both San Diego and Oakland. He had retired in 1965, but we constantly teased him about coming out of retirement—and he loved every minute of it. In his mind, he'll be playing football for the rest of his life.

Hoot was an original "high-sider." During our special team meetings, the blacks would always needle him, telling him to wise up and realize that he was white and he just shouldn't be high-siding and styling like some flashy brother. When he played in Oakland, he would wait to receive the kickoffs, his head cocked to the side and his shoulder leaning casually against the goal post, with one leg up on the post. The announcer would call the name "Claude Gibson," and the crowd would yell, "Hoot, Hoot." Then he would put on his act, striding out with his knees up to his chest and his arms pumping while the crowd cheered. He would wind up with a big bow and go back to wait for the kick—and the crowd was crazy about him even when he didn't break loose for a long return. He loved to show us that act during our own drills, and we all praised him for his styling. And if he ever happened to get his hands on the ball in practice, he would take off on a twisting runback. He had the enthusiasm of a young kid, and it rubbed off. He was a great guy to have around.

If Hoot was more of a player than a coach to us, then Preston Ridlehuber balanced the situation by acting more like a coach than a player. For a guy who'd never really made it in pro ball, Preston thought he knew more about football than any star. From the day he walked into practice, he began instructing James Harris on how to throw and telling me how to hit the holes. One day he spent a lot of time advising the receivers on how to catch the ball. Then he ran a pattern of his own; the ball came right to him and he dropped it. "That's the way, Coach Ridlehuber," said Maguire. "If you stop coaching, maybe you'll catch the ball next time." Even Coach Rauch had to laugh, and from that day on, Ridlehuber was known as The Coach.

Ridlehuber was funny to watch because he had a knock-kneed style of running that made him wiggle all over when he headed into the open field. Maguire and some of the other guys did good imitations of Preston's running and everybody got a lot of laughs—but that never stopped him from giving out advice and telling stories. He claimed to know just about everything there was to know about pro ball.

Once somebody happened to be talking about Alex Hawkins, the running back and special-team star who had played for Baltimore and Atlanta. "I taught Alex a lot about playing on special teams," said Preston. "I roomed with him when I was with Atlanta."

"The other day," Maguire interrupted, "you said that you roomed with somebody else on Atlanta. And two days before that, you were telling stories about still another roommate. Did you switch rooms every night when you tried out for the Falcons."

"Well," Ridlehuber explained slowly. "We were all sort of roommates. At least, we all stayed in the same dormitory."

When the deer-hunting season arrived, a number of the Bills began to go hunting after practice. Ridlehuber took one look at their guns, and came up with a deer-hunting story of his own. "I couldn't count the deer I've shot," he said. "But I'll never forget the first one I ever killed because the poor thing actually died in my arms."

Everyone started to break up over that, but he went on, with a dead-serious look on his face. "The deer was following me home down a little trail in the woods. Suddenly I turned around, and it jumped with fright. There was a high cliff right behind it and it plunged off the edge. I scrambled down and held it in my lap as it died."

After hearing that one, the guys were determined to make up a story that Ridlehuber couldn't top. Finally Mc-Dole said, "Hey Coach, did you hear what Jim Dunaway did once?"

"What?" asked Ridlehuber, his mind already working on some wild story to reply with.

"He killed two deer with one shot."

"Were they California deer or Mississippi deer?"

"What the hell difference does that make."

"California deer are smaller," Preston said. "Anybody can kill two of them with one shot."

I got some free coaching from another source after the Cincinnati game. We won, 16-13, but Paul Robinson, the Rookie of the Year of 1968, had his best day of the season in the driving blizzard, slipping through and around tacklers for 117 yards. That apparently made him feel pretty good because afterwards he said, "That Simpson will be a pretty good back, but he dances too much behind the line of scrimmage. He'll have to learn to start hitting the holes more quickly."

His statement surprised me because Robinson had been having a bad year; in fact, our game was his first 100-yard game of the season—and they hadn't won it, anyway. Paul Costa reminded me of an article he had shown me earlier in the year in which Robinson had said, "O.J. should do well, but whatever else he gets, he won't take the rushing title away from me." Now after twelve games, he was far behind me in rushing, and he still wanted to give me tips. If he had been Dickie Post, who was leading the league, I would have accepted anything he had to say. But Robinson had nothing to boast about for the year. I felt like making a few choice comments about the number of yards he'd made all season, but I decided it would be smarter to keep quiet. When someone asked me about his comments, I just said, "Who won the game?"

The game itself was just a snowy blur to me afterward. My hands froze, my face smarted, and I could barely see where I was going in the blizzard. At half time the trainer stuck my hands in some hot wax to bring the feeling back to them; when it was time to go back out onto the field, he peeled the wax off and I could move my fingers again for a while. After the game my hands ached so badly that I wanted to just hold them under hot water and rub them, but Kemp came into the shower and told me not to do it. He said that I should just let them thaw out gradually so I wouldn't do them any permanent harm.

We mixed our running and passing pretty well to control the ball, but the only statistic that mattered was that the Bengals fumbled seven times and we recovered all seven. The biggest play came when Booker stole the ball from Greg Cook and ran it into the end zone. Added to three field goals by Bruce Alford in the tricky wind, it was enough to bring us the victory.

I gained 35 yards, but let a touchdown get away from me when I tried to shove the ball over the goal line after one run—only to have it slip out of my frozen fingers. The kickoff–return title also slid away from me that day. The field was so bad that every Cincinnati kick bounced on the ice at about our twenty, and by the time I scrambled around and picked the ball up, I got nailed each time. After three of those plays, my last chance to lead the AFL in any category was gone.

Once my hands thawed out, I felt happy enough about the victory. I couldn't help feeling that we could have whipped the Bengals more impressively on a decent field; but when you're 4-8, you probably shouldn't complain about any game you're fortunate enough to win. The postgame party at the hotel was livelier than I would have expected; I gathered that the Buffalo veterans were accustomed to playing—and winning—under blizzard conditions. In fact, years of handling Buffalo winters had produced a special pride in some of our elder players; they shrugged off the weather and let the visiting team—and rookies like me—worry about little things like frozen hands. As Cincinnati coach Paul Brown said after the game, "Under these conditions, it's the hard-bitten professionals who produce." Whatever our weaknesses, we certainly had plenty of tough old pros.

I learned some terrible news that week. I hadn't seen much of Bob James because I was hustling around getting ready to leave town and he was rushing home from practice to see his wife, who was due to have their baby at any time. For the last few weeks of the season, I even stopped rooming with Bob on the nights before our games. Booker and Wayne Patrick had been rooming next to us, and we all realized that Booker and I both liked to watch television and stay up late talking, while Wingate and Robert grabbed all the sleep they could. So we had switched, and when Booker and I didn't see Bob on the night before the Cincinnati game, we just assumed that he was up in his room taking an early nap. Then somebody told us. Bob had called the coach and said that he would be reporting late. His wife had lost the baby.

He arrived at the hotel late that night and stopped in the coffee shop to eat. I went down to talk to him, but when I got there, I realized that I didn't know what the hell to say. He seemed remarkably calm, almost in a daze. The pain was visible in his eyes, but his mouth curled in a determined expression; as always, Robert was trying to pull himself together to do his job on the field the next day. Looking into his face, I realized how close

I had grown to Robert. I had argued and joked with him, and talked a lot about how much he had changed during the season. But the changes hadn't affected his basic personality. He was still a dedicated, sincere individual who lived his life strictly by the rules. No one worked harder; no one tried more consistently to do what he believed was the right thing. Personal tragedies always seem unfair and senseless. But this one hit me especially hard because if anyone deserved some good things in return for the way he lived, it was Bob James. On the surface, I had felt that I had broadened his life by making him more sophisticated and less hung-up on his country background. But sitting with him that night, I realized that beneath the surface, he had broadened my life just as much. Knowing him had been a rich part of my education.

My final days in Buffalo seemed to fly past me. Our practices for the game in Kansas City were crisp and uneventful, and the team headed into our concluding road trip in high spirits. It was funny to think that the season was virtually over. I recalled pulling into the dusty driveway of my apartment building for the first time and thinking, "My God, three months in Buffalo. This will seem like an eternity." But now the three months were over, and they had been crowded with new experiences and emotions; I had barely noticed them going by.

In a strange way, I even felt some regrets about leaving Buffalo. During those closing weeks, the members of our club had finally gotten to know one another. We all stopped trying to play roles or hide our real feelings. And as we began to show our emotions openly, we were inevitably drawn closer together. I remembered what Paul Costa had said at McDole's Halloween party about what a waste it was to complain about being in Buffalo. He was right in so many ways. I had spent too much time, for instance, looking forward to rejoining my old USC teammates in California. They were good friends, but the fact was that the Bills would be my teammates for much longer than my junior college or college friends. My future happiness, and my success as a player, would depend on my teammates in Buffalo, and I was sorry I hadn't devoted myself more completely to understanding them. As I did finally begin to know them well, I felt genuinely sorry about leaving them; I resolved to keep in touch with as many as I could during the off-season.

Ironically, our very last days in Buffalo were bright and sunny. The temperature rose, the snow melted, and getting to southern California no longer seemed so important. Our plane left Buffalo on a beautiful afternoon; peering out the window, I actually felt a little sad—and a bit anxious to get back the next fall and start working there again.

A few hours later we landed in Kansas City. The first snowstorm of the season was just beginning there.

Chapter Nineteen

The Future Champs

Buffalo teams have always played well against Kansas City, and going into our second game against the Chiefs, we had several special incentives. The defensive players, in particular, were still angry over the timeout that Hank Stram had called with three seconds left in our first game; Harry Jacobs talked all week about how much he wanted to upset the Chiefs and make Stram regret that last touchdown he had rolled up against us. In addition, the Houston Oilers were stumbling so badly that, as ridiculous as it may have seemed, we still had a shot at second place and a playoff spot. It would have taken an almost incredible set of results to shove us ahead of both Houston and Boston—but when the Oilers lost badly to the Jets the day before our Kansas City game, we couldn't help but feel a faint glimmer of hope.

We kept that hope alive until the final minutes of the game. It was another bruising, all-out struggle that we had every reason to be proud of. To a lot of people around the AFL, we may have been just another set of also-rans; but if you ask the Chiefs, they'll tell you that Buffalo could

be as tough as any club in the league. We could have upset them twice, in fact, if it hadn't been for the incredible
field goal kicking of Jan Stenerud. During a five-week
period, Stenerud set a pro record with sixteen consecu-
tive field goals; the first five and the last five in his streak
came in the two games against us. In that second game,
he kicked them from as far as 52 and 47 yards to help
the Chiefs open a 16-6 lead in what could have been a
low-scoring defensive deadlock. When we fought back
to tie the game at 19-19 in the last quarter, Stenerud
kicked his fifth of the day to win it, 22-19.

Kemp had a good day; he didn't pass for a lot of yardage but he avoided interceptions and controlled the ball
fairly well. Our whole offense had a good afternoon
against the Chiefs, who have a defense that is huge, quick,
and very hard to read—as Joe Kapp and the Vikings
found out in the Super Bowl. In the fourth quarter, when
we were down, 19-13, we showed an ability to make the
big plays that had been lacking all year. Jack hit me with
a swing pass and I broke loose for 19 yards. Then he hit
Bobby Crockett, a receiver who was playing his first game
for us, with a 15-yard pass over the middle. Two of those
big Chief linebackers were thundering toward him as the
pass arrived, but Crockett held on to it. In fact, it was
his fourth catch of the day, and every one was in heavy
traffic on slant patterns over the middle.

Crockett was twenty-six years old, and he had missed
almost three years of regular action with knee and ankle
injuries; I had no idea where he fit into Coach Rauch's
plans for the future. But during that game I became one
of Bobby's biggest admirers. I had run enough slant patterns to know how much courage they demanded—and
Crockett had to be the most courageous receiver I had
ever seen. Every time he went into the game, it seemed

that the play was a pass over the middle. And somehow he battled his way through the linebackers and got to the right spot; several of his catches were sensational.

Few fans realize how much guts a back or an end needs to run one of those slants in pro football. Yet if there were any moments at which I had any doubts at all about my willingness to take punishment on the football field, they came on those patterns. College linebackers generally have different assignments than the pros; they are not as totally dedicated to making sure that a back or end doesn't violate their territory. But the best pro linebackers consider it as a personal affront if you try to cut across the middle for a pass. And so they will clothesline you, crack you with a forearm, and do anything else to make you regret your invasion of their area; even if you catch a pass in that territory, you usually get a few bruises to remember it by.

To illustrate the effects of slant patterns, look at a team like the Miami Dolphins. For several years, everybody has said that the Dolphins would be a great passing team if their receivers were fast and healthy enough to catch Bob Griese's passes. But there was a reason why their receivers were always crippled or slowed by injuries; under Coach George Wilson's system, they ran an incredible amount of slant patterns. Our linebackers knew this, and so did every other linebacker in the league. Everybody would just lay in wait for those poor suckers, knowing that they'd be coming over the middle; when they did, they often wound up getting hurt. I felt sorry for a guy like Jim Hines, the Olympic 100-meter champion who was laughed at and nicknamed "Oops" because he dropped so many passes in Miami. I didn't know if Jim would have made it with any club, but I knew that those Miami pass patterns had to be the hardest in football for a converted track star to master. Even after all my football experience,

I still listened for the footsteps of a Butkus or a Buoniconti on a few slant plays; I imagined how those footsteps
must have been echoing in Hines's ears.

Crockett's gutsy catch, on the Chiefs' thirty-two-yard-line,
might have given the whole team a small lift because on
the next play we executed a sweep as perfectly as we had
all season. I took the ball to the outside and saw Billy
Shaw and Joe O'Donnell in front of me. They really nailed
two defenders, and I went all the way to tie the game. The
extra point would have put us ahead.

But we didn't make it. A high pass from center broke
up the play, and Briscoe, the holder, could only try a futile
pass that fell incomplete. It was just one of a number of
small mistakes that meant the difference between the
good football team that we had become and the winning
team that we should have been. Wingate and I each fumbled once to set up field goals by Stenerud; we used our
timeouts early in the second half and didn't have any
when we needed them in the final minutes; we drew key
penalties that stalled two drives in Kansas City territory.
And so we lost a game that we probably deserved to win,
and for all practical purposes, our season was finished.

For the Chiefs, on the other hand, the season was virtually starting all over. They were in second place, a game
behind the Raiders in the Western Division. They had to
face the Raiders in Oakland on the final Saturday of the
season; win or lose, they would go on to the playoffs. I
never would have predicted at the time that a month later,
I would be watching them destroy Minnesota in the Super
Bowl. I was convinced that Oakland would be the Super
Bowl champion.

The Chiefs had a lot going for them, to be sure. In our
two games against them, I hadn't seen all their weapons
because Len Dawson had been out of the lineup three-

quarters of the time, and Mike Livingston, his replacement, had two poor days against us. But you had to respect their running attack, their receivers, their offensive line, and their depth; and playing on offense, I gained a special respect for their defense. Bobby Bell, the left linebacker, was as tough and fast as anyone I'd faced; he was one of the few defenders whom I hadn't handled fairly easily in one-on-one situations in the open field. Willie Lanier was another star, a smart and rugged ballplayer who was disproving once and for all the racist rumors that a black couldn't be a middle linebacker; Willie not only played the position brilliantly, but he called the signals for one of the most complicated defensive systems in football.

The Kansas City defensive line was awesome. Their pass defense was not quite as perfect as Oakland's, but the line put so much pressure on passers that cornerbacks Emmitt Thomas and Jim Marsalis could afford to play a tight, gambling style. The Chiefs' tackles, Buck Buchanan and Curly Culp, made it almost impossible to break through the middle on running plays; end Aaron Brown was one of the fastest in football, and Jerry Mays was a tough and tricky veteran. Nobody who played against the Chiefs could have been too surprised when their offensive and defensive linemen completely outplayed the more publicized Vikings.

Yet I didn't think that the Chiefs would make it to the Super Bowl, and many other players around the league felt the same way. Their talent was unquestioned, but their many stars didn't always play together. To put it bluntly, they were considered front runners. The word was, get a jump on them early and they'll fall apart. When they could control the pace of the game and grind an opponent down with their running attack, they would win; but when things began to go badly for them and they needed a big play, they didn't always get it. In addition, they didn't seem able to rise to big games. Some thought that their system was so complicated that just concentrating on the plays required so much attention that there was no room left for emotion; talking to some of their players, I also got the feeling that the Chiefs weren't the happiest club around. Whatever the reason, at that point the Raiders, a team that always stuck together under pressure, seemed to have Kansas City's number. They had won six of their last seven games with the Chiefs.

The Raiders made it seven out of eight the next week with a 10-6 victory. It was a strange game in which Stram had the Chiefs do nothing but run the ball—and Raider defenders like Tom Keating and Dan Conners stopped them over and over with big tackles. I thought that the running strategy might have been a sign of desperation, and I believed that the Chiefs would be knocked off by the Jets in the first playoff game. There was no doubt that the Chiefs were a better team; the Jets' pass defense was one of the weakest in the league. But Namath usually made the big plays, and I thought somehow he would upset the Chiefs.

It was the Kansas City defense, however, that came up with the biggest plays of the season over the next three weeks. They smothered Namath and the Jets, 13-6, and they finally upset the Raiders, 17-7, aided by an injury that made Daryle Lamonica ineffective for most of the game. I had been dead wrong about the Chiefs—and so had many AFL players. They had at last gotten together for some big games, and in the biggest game of all, the Super Bowl, they came up with their best effort.

After playing the Chiefs twice, I had to smile at some

of the things Minnesota tried to do against them. The Vikings actually thought that their big backs could run inside against Buchanan and Culp; and they thought that their cornerbacks could play from 8 to 10 yards away from the line and concede a receiver like Otis Taylor the short pass. Buck and Culp punished them all day for their arrogance—and Otis burned them by turning one 4-yard pass into a 50-yard touchdown that clinched the game.

In the two playoff games and the Super Bowl, the Chiefs had allowed a total of two touchdowns; that made me proud that we had moved the ball so well in our second game against them. But everybody in the AFL felt a more general sense of pride after that Super Bowl. In the last game before the merger ended the separate existence of the AFL, the old myth of NFL superiority had been completely shattered. If anything, the AFL was years ahead in techniques. In fact, I still thought that Oakland would have whipped the Vikings by an even more lopsided score; and I felt that the Jets would have beaten Minnesota, too. For all their weaknesses, they would have scored an awful lot of points; Namath just eats up pass defenses like Minnesota's.

It was nice to feel a part of the superior league, and it was also ironic. I remembered how much I had hoped to play in the NFL. Growing up in San Francisco and playing in L.A., I had believed the NFL myths as completely as anybody. Crashing into players like Bell and Buoniconti every week had quickly cured me of any ideas that the AFL was a weaker league, but I knew that there were a lot of diehards who would keep believing the NFL propagandists until they were proven wrong beyond doubt. Namath had provided the first jolt to those people by upsetting Baltimore in 1969; but many still claimed that Joe was just one superstar and didn't represent the quality of a whole league. The Chiefs, however, were a team that had to battle just to survive in the AFL. They had lost to Cincinnati, beaten us by three points—and finished second in their division. They had strengths and weaknesses, hot streaks and slumps that made them very representative of our league. And no one could have asked for better representation last January in New Orleans.

Chapter Twenty

Getting It Over With

Our last game in San Diego isn't worth describing. If you were lucky enough not to see it, you're better off to be left in ignorance. We were just pitiful. It wasn't a question of making mistakes or messing up plays. We simply didn't hit, didn't execute—didn't play football. The score was 45-6, but it didn't give a true indication of how bad we were.

To say that the game was an anticlimax is really no excuse. As professionals, we should have been able to go out and put on a good performance no matter how meaningless the game was. But we were in a strange mental state. For six weeks we had been working harder, communicating better, and becoming a football team. It had been an emotional period, and our emotions had peaked in those moments when we were on the verge of upsetting Kansas City. Then we had lost the game and been eliminated from any chance of making the playoffs—and the emotions had been sapped from us. Some top teams can have a flat week and still play a good, workmanlike game. But we weren't good enough to get away with that. We paid dearly for our letdown.

For the first time in over a month, there was grumbling on the club during our stay in San Diego. Watching the game films, we were impressed again by the fearless Bobby Crockett as he went for passes over the middle. I watched him get clotheslined on one play and I cringed. But Coach Rauch wasn't moved by his courage. "Bobby," he said, "you're letting those guys get too good a shot at you."

The coach may have been right; if you let yourself get hit too often on those plays, you'll get hurt. Yet he hadn't said a word about the great catches Bobby had made— and then he picked out one play and criticized him for it. Crockett was pretty upset. "You'd think he could have said 'Nice catch' or something," he said, "before he started knocking me. Every time I went in, I ran that same play. Sure I got belted a few times, but I also caught four passes. He could have mentioned that."

A number of the guys agreed with him, and it was a topic of conversation for several days. For our workouts, we had to walk about half a mile from our motel; on those walks it seemed that everybody was talking about Crockett and the coach. Rauch was the kind of man who believed in letting you know when you made a mistake; when you did something good, he seldom got enthusiastic. That was just his style, and it hadn't especially bothered me. But the Crockett case got a lot of us annoyed. Every football player respects somebody with exceptional guts. And Bobby had shown all the guts in the world, only to have the coach say, "You got necktied. You shouldn't have done it that way."

To try to keep us on edge for the game, Coach Rauch also announced that we would have an eleven o'clock curfew every night of the week. That caused a lot of trouble. The veterans were most insulted, saying that they were grown men who didn't have to be tucked into bed

every night. There was a lot of talk about purposely staying out late and defying the coach, and for a while it
appeared that it could be an explosive issue. Finally the
guys got together and decided to approach the coach about
it. Harry Jacobs, Maguire, and a few others formed a committee to talk to him. I wondered if the confrontation
would produce a lot of bad feelings.

But the coach listened to the guys very quietly and said,
"Maybe you're right. I didn't think about it that way. Let's
hold off on the curfew until later in the week." The reaction was unexpected and it moved Rauch up in the opinions of many of us. As cold as he may have seemed
at times, he proved that he was truly willing to listen to
us and consider our viewpoints. It was something that
didn't sink in to some of us until the season was almost
gone, but it will mean a lot next year when we begin playing for him again. That gesture ended the complaining
for the week, and our basically good mood returned.

Unfortunately, we did nothing to show our apprecia-
tion to Rauch. We played as if we had stayed out all
night every night of the week. Actually, we had worked
fairly hard for the game. But we couldn't shake the flat
feeling that had set in after the Kansas City game. We
felt relaxed and happy, but we just didn't feel like playing football. And so we ended the season on a very low
note.

In the aftermath of that San Diego farce, you couldn't
help but look at the worst aspects of our season. Our
record was 4-10, which might have seemed to be a decent
improvement over the 1-12-1 of the year before. Yet our
four wins had come over a Denver team playing without
Floyd Little and Steve Tensi; a Boston team in the midst
of a seven-game losing streak of its own; a Miami team
without Bob Griese and Nick Buoniconti; and a Cincinnati

team in a blizzard. Against the four teams that wound up in the AFL playoffs, we had gone 0-7. We had also gone 0-7 on the road.

There was no doubt that we had some players who weren't putting out to the fullest. We had genuine old pros like Billy Shaw, Joe O'Donnell, Ron McDole, and Jim Dunaway, and we had a number of young guys who were really determined to make the Bills into a winner. But we also had some athletes who were just hanging on to pick up those weekly checks. Winning and losing didn't seem to matter to them; they had lost their competitive feeling. Those players would have to be weeded out and replaced before we could fulfill our potential—and younger men would have to fill in with a new spirit of eagerness. But Coach Rauch made it clear that he planned to weed out some veterans, and we had enough youth to supply all the enthusiasm he needed for the future.

Hours after the San Diego game, I was on a plane for Las Vegas with Booker, Marlin, and Charley Ferguson. We wanted to get our minds as far from the game as possible so we could go home and start the off-season with a fresh perspective. We gambled and lost some money, we saw some shows, and enjoyed some good food. But by the time I went home, I realized that I didn't really want to get my mind off football. I was already looking forward to the start of the next season.

Chapter Twenty-One

Looking Ahead

Shortly after the end of the season, I helped broadcast the East–West Shrine Game in San Francisco for ABC. On the morning of the game, I was walking through the hotel lobby when I heard a voice call, "Hey, O.J." I turned and saw Coach Rauch—and I was genuinely happy to see him. A few months earlier, I never would have guessed that I'd give a damn about chatting with Rauch during the off-season. He had been Satan to us, yelling orders and criticisms and remaining aloof. Yet on that morning, only a few weeks after I had left him, I greeted him like a long-lost friend. We talked for a while about the college players he was scouting and our prospects for next year; he was very interested in how I was doing, and I was anxious to hear about his plans. When he finally walked away, the vague trends that had been building since midseason became clear in my mind. The harsh words and bitter feelings of the past began to seem very minor. Coach Rauch and I had at last achieved a feeling of mutual respect and mutual purpose; we were communicating freely, uninhibited by our personal differences. We were friends. It was the kind of feeling that I got when

I met Marv Goux of USC—a feeling that made me more
anxious than ever to start playing for Coach Rauch again.

When I left the coach, I realized for the first time that
I already missed the guys back in Buffalo. Booker had
stayed with me for a few days when we came home from
Vegas, and Haven had come up from San Diego for dinner; but I suddenly wished that I could see more of all
the Bills. I hadn't realized until that day that, in all the
joking and the anger of the hectic season, we had formed
some strong relationships. Like every kind of education,
my rookie year had produced effects that I hadn't even
been conscious of—until it was over and I could look
back on it.

At the AFL All-Star game in Houston, I had a long talk
with Harry Jacobs. At times, Harry and I had seemed to
be living in different worlds. Our ages and our approaches
to football had kept us far apart. But in Houston, I learned
that Harry had been trying as hard as I had to bridge the
generation gap on the Bills. He admitted that he had
made some mistakes in dealing with people during the
season, and I told him that I regretted some of the things
I'd done. "You're a big factor in the future of our club,"
he told me. "I know being a rookie held you back from
expressing yourself at times, but next year, I hope you'll
take over as one of the team's leaders."

"I plan to try," I said. "If we work together instead of
separately, maybe we can bring the two age groups together, once and for all."

"If we do, we'll be a very different kind of team." Harry
spoke in his uniquely sincere way, and his face showed
that he had benefited greatly from some of the troubles
we'd gone through. As I had suggested in my first weeks
in camp, we had all been rookies in a sense; and the really
dedicated veterans—Harry and Billy Shaw and the others
—had learned almost as much from our stormy, emo-

tional season as I had. We'll all be better off for it next
year.

The Bills selected Al Cowlings as their first choice in the
draft. After teasing me all season about how I was over-
rating Cowlings, Harve Johnson had picked him as the
fourth-best player available. I was delighted that Al would
be joining me in Buffalo; it will be great to have him
around again, and he'll bring new speed and life to our
defensive line. In fact, Al was only one of several young
players who promised to give the Bills a new look.

Our veteran defense will be back, but it should get even
stronger as men like Al, Edgar Chandler, and Bob James
try to fight their way into the lineup. On offense, Billy
Shaw and Joe O'Donnell, who both came off major injuries last year, may be even stronger; and young blockers
like Angelo Loukas and Mike Richey will give some
needed spark to our offensive line. If Ben Gregory re-
covers fully from his knee problems, we'll be loaded with
running backs. And if he stays healthy, James Harris has
simply got to become a top quarterback.

But the major changes won't be in personnel. We will
be thinking like a different team. The personal wars of
last season will become a collective struggle; the unity
that was forged over the last half of the 1969 season will
be with us from the first day of training camp. You can't
just give a speech or clap your hands and pull a team
together. It takes suffering and pain and a long time; and
we went through it all last season.

I'll be a different ballplayer, too. Physically, I'll be in
my best condition from the start. I'm still committed to
auto shows, speaking engagements, and television during
the off-season, but most of all, I'm committed to the Bills.
Days after the season ended, I started regular workouts
at USC with Al and Mike Taylor. And I'll keep it up right

through the summer. A year ago I was overwhelmed by the sheer magnitude of the business opportunities ahead of me; in the excitement and confusion, I let myself drift through the off-season. The hardest thing in the world for a poor kid who suddenly becomes a rich and busy businessman is to keep things in perspective. I lost that perspective for a while, and it took some crushing tackles and bitter disappointments to jolt everything back into place for me. It was a rugged lesson that I don't want to go through twice; business won't get in the way of football anymore.

My emotional state will also be altered. Last year I was always mad about something. I wanted to run the ball more, I wanted to be back in California, I wanted to do things my own way. That kind of anger can't help you in football. It can only detract from the intense concentration that an athlete needs every time he executes a play. This year every ounce of my emotions will go into slamming into the holes faster and harder than I've ever done before. And what's left over will be poured out to my teammates—not in anger but in enthusiasm. I'm going to live up to my promise to Harry Jacobs. I'm going to help lead the Bills to the top.

Carl Garrett won the coaches' poll for Rookie of the Year, and Greg Cook was the sportswriters' selection. I didn't come close, although I gained a few more yards rushing and receiving than Garrett. That was understandable because people had expected great things from me, and I had fallen far short. Even if I had backed into the Rookie title because it was a poor year for rookies, it wouldn't have meant very much. I didn't go into the season looking for a trophy; I was trying to live up to the image I had built. I wanted to give people the touchdowns and thrills that they expected of me, and I wanted to make the Bills into a winner. When I couldn't do those things, consolation prizes didn't matter.

In some ways, my reputation survived the season intact. After our shameful performance in San Diego, everybody had a right to be disgusted. And yet people still crowded around me in the locker room, anxious to interview me and wish me well. And even in the postseason summaries of my performances, very few people wrote me off as a major disappointment. Many athletes have endured much rougher treatment, and I was grateful for the faith and patience people showed toward me. Being a rich rookie was a difficult experience, but it could have been much worse without that support.

Next year I'm going to pay everybody back for their patience. And it will be just as satisfying as it would have been to tear the league apart last year. In a sense, it may even be better. Until last year, everything had been easy for me on a football field. Now I know the other side of the sport. And that knowledge can only make success that much sweeter.

In the second round of the college draft, the Bills selected Dennis Shaw, the quarterback from San Diego State. He was rated as one of the three or four best quarterbacks in the country, and he'll certainly find a good opportunity with the Bills. Jack Kemp has announced that he will run for Congress, and will probably retire; even if he stays in football, Jack won't be the quarterback Rauch wants to build around for the future. That role will fall to Harris, Darragh, or Shaw—and if they stay healthy, their battle for the job will help all of us.

Shaw called me after the draft and asked if he could come up and work out with us some time at USC; he sounded very enthusiastic about starting pro ball. Then

I started reading the statements he was making to the press. He talked about how much money he was worth, how much he could do for the Bills, and how he expected no trouble adjusting from college to professional football. The remarks were hauntingly familiar; I had said the same things a year before. For a moment I felt like calling Shaw back and telling him, "Cool it. Don't build up too many hopes. You're only going to make things harder for yourself."

But I didn't call. Who was I to tell him what to say? And would he have listened to me anyway? Probably not. He was just a rookie. And rookies have to get their education the hard way.